WORSHIP IN OUR FAMILY

Paul W. Henshaw
&
Harold E. Weemhoff, Jr.

illustrated by Nancy G. Johnstone

THE UPPER ROOM
Nashville, Tennessee

WORSHIP IN OUR FAMILY

The material in this book first appeared in a series of articles in the *Christian Home* magazine.

Book design by Nancy G. Johnstone
First printing: July 1981 (5)
Library of Congress Catalog Card No.: 81-52045
ISBN: 0-8358-0421-6
Printed in the United States of America

WORSHIP IN OUR FAMILY

We would like to dedicate this book
to our own families and to the families
within the local congregations,
both past and present,
who have taught us to worship.

CONTENTS

INTRODUCTION

The worship services that follow are very personal and private kinds of sharing from us. They represent our own understanding of what it means to be a family at worship, and they document our own struggles to find appropriate ways to express the faith we share. For us, worship is the way we discover God and rehearse the drama of our own lives together so that we remember *who* and *whose* we are. It is most appropriate, then, that this expression of who and whose we are is performed within the context of our own families and within our own homes. These are the persons that matter the most to us; this is the place where we struggle to grow and mature, and where we finally discover life at its fullest. It is in the context of the home and family that we first learn what it means to be loved and respected and trusted. From these human relationships we discover and understand our relationship with God. It is with family members that we learn about failing and guilt and forgiveness and acceptance. Our interpretation of God and how we respond to God is clarified in our family living. We worship constantly in our everyday struggles to live with one another as a family, but we often do not recognize the worship aspects of our daily lives together.

Well, what is worship? Originally, the word was used as a title to designate someone who was important—someone who was *someone:* "Your Worship." In many ways, that same understanding applies today. Worship is the time when we recognize that we are *someone;* it is the time when we thank God for what he has done and the time when we are enabled to become the person God created us to be. Stop and think for a moment about the implications of what you have just read.

We are saying that we accept ourselves and others as important because we worship a God who has created us and wants us to show our love for him by loving other people. It is through worship of God that we recognize and praise God as our Creator and that we pray to God for ourselves and for others. Because we are creations of a loving and concerned God, we know we are worthwhile and capable of loving. We are *someone* because of God and God's love for us.

Worship is the time when we tell our story: the story we love to tell and need to tell. The story explains how God loves and sustains us. It is in worship that we recognize that we belong to God, we hear the good news that God loves and sustains us, and we respond to the good news by loving others. In worship we get in touch with our God, the power and strength that is beyond us and greater than we are. Because of what God has done throughout history and has done in our lives, we respond in love. We come into God's presence to praise God, to confess before God, to be renewed by God, and to be sent out to serve God. Because of God, we are people of worth.

If we are *someones* in our family settings of worship, what does this say about our style of family worship? We hope it says that our worship is first and foremost *celebration.* It is joyful. It is pleasurable. It is fun. It is exciting. It is challenging. It is motivating. It means that each member of the family participates in it equally, and every person, no matter how young or old, is seen as important for planning and celebrating the worship event.

Also this idea of worship means that we can all learn from each other and that even the youngest child can and must lead worship moments in our families. No one automatically assumes the leadership of worship. We share worship together, just as we share life together. Each of us learns and teaches one another, and each of us assumes different roles in relationship to one another.

Worship is action. It is not just the words that we say, but more importantly, it is the action that we perform. It is the way that we respond to God's love. It is the way in which we say to our family members and others that each of us counts, each of us is important, each of us is *someone* because God created each of us and loves each of us!

The words without the action are meaningless. How can we be joyful and celebrate with a frown or an angry expression on our faces? Children learn by what we do, not what we say. Worship is our doing *for God;* it is our time to show through our actions that each of us is of worth, both to God and to one another. Too often we believe good worship depends upon what we say and how we say it. We are embarrassed and fearful about any worship experience (even grace before meals or bedtime prayers) because we don't know the right words or are afraid we will appear silly or stupid. But the words matter so little! The emphasis in worship is on the action: on how we act out what we believe and say. We worship best and most eloquently when we demonstrate our love and concern for God's world or one of God's creatures or another person. That is what worship is all about. This is how we praise God and respond to God's love and care in our own lives.

What we are really trying to say is that family worship is not a rushed, confusing five-minute exercise that we force the family to endure. Rather, it is a time when the family really comes together, a time when the family is focused on what family is all about, a time when the family is centered and given direction and reminded of its purpose and true values. It is hoped that the worship times together can be an opportunity to focus the family and center the life of the family on what it means to be children of God and *someones* of worth to God and others. In reality, worship is not a five-minute activity, but it is daily living together as a family; it is the honest sharing of life, both its joys and successes and its concerns and disappointments. True family worship is the action we share with one another as we live together; it is the getting ready to celebrate and the cleaning up after the daily celebration. Worship is the carry-over for the rest of the day's activities. We would like you to see family worship as you do three meals a day: spread worship out and depend on it, as you do your meals. These special moments—sacred, if you will—these treasured moments together help us to clarify and define who we are and who we hope to become in our families.

Let's leave the "oughts," the "shoulds," and the "musts" out of this family tradition. If we view worship as something that we ought to do or must do occasionally so that we don't feel guilty, our children will surely know this, and instead of our entire family life being centered in worship (in our belief that we are *someones*), family worship will be seen as a chore or task to be endured. We are saying that everything counts for family worship. It has to be personal and uniquely your own family celebration, but your family probably needs resources and ideas and guidelines. That is the intention of these materials. This is a collection of resources for parents and leaders of worship. It can be of value for church school teachers and for workers with children, but its primary purpose is to supply families with resources for creating their own celebrations together. We have provided the system, the resources, and a structure. Now test that system with your own family's life-style. Decide what you like and what you do not like. Decide what works for you and what does not. Experiment! Try some of the ideas on! The selections in this book will contain many different suggestions. Decide as a family which days you want to celebrate and how you want to celebrate them.

You might want to talk about establishing a worship center for your family. We don't mean a formal shrine, but rather a place where you gather materials for these family celebrations and where you might center your family's worship activity. It might be on the refrigerator door or on top of the television set or in the center of the kitchen table or even in one of the children's rooms (the children could take turns hosting the family worship moments in their rooms if you choose to celebrate right before the children go to bed). The importance of establishing a worship center is that it will focus your family's attention on what you are doing and will remind everyone who passes the center during the days ahead of what took place there and why you came as a family to worship. If a member of your family is absent from the worship event (he or she might be on a trip or away at college or ill, or dad or mom may be away on business), place a picture of that person on the worship center so that all of you who do gather there will remember the missing family member. It will help the missing person to know that he or she is included in the worship moments, even though he or she is absent.

Just a word about the structure of each worship activity. You will find a section entitled **Preparation,** a section called **Worship,** a list of ideas called **Living Our Worship,** and a section called **Remembrances.**

Preparation should help you and your children to discover why we selected that day for celebration. It is designed to focus your thinking on the importance of the day for us as human beings, as Americans, and, most important, as Christians. Some of the background, historical insights, and biblical references will be included in this **Preparation.** We suggest that both parents and children share this material together. If your children are too young to read, read the section to them and then talk about why we celebrate on this special day. We have found that as we prepared this section it was sometimes difficult to get at the real reason for the celebration and the true significance of the day or event. This section is an attempt at answering the young child's constant question, "Why?"

The **Worship** resources will be based on the worship experience of Isaiah found in Isaiah 6:1-8. Worship resources will always contain four elements: adoration, confession, affirmation, and dedication. In the element of adoration, we praise God for who he is and thank God for what he has done in our lives. We acknowledge that God is at work in all of the world. Through confession, we come to a better understanding of ourselves and who we are meant to be. The affirmation time is an opportunity to grow in faith and to share with one another what is important to us as individuals and as a family unit. It is in the dedication section that we declare our acceptance of new life and our action to show both ourselves and others *who* and *whose* we are. This element is our response to God.

The third section is entitled **Living Our Worship** and contains ideas and suggestions about activities that would help all the family members better to understand and live their worship moments together. We see this section as really crucial because it will supply the ideas for action in our worship. The words of the service will not be as helpful if they are not coupled with one of the action ideas included in this section. We hope that each of you can find some appropriate idea in this section that appeals to you and enables you to *live* your worship event. Much of the real worship experience will be enhanced and made real by the planning and preparation for using one or more of these suggestions. It is vital that all of you, no matter how young, be involved in selecting which of the ideas you wish to use. If you cannot agree on one idea, certainly some members of the family could work on several suggestions.

In **Remembrances,** we have made suggestions for helping to clarify and reinforce the basic ideas in the worship resources for the day. **Remembrances** will make suggestions about how to help your family keep the moments of celebration alive and ways for you as a parent or adult to understand what a child learned or understood from the moments of worship.

A word about how to use this book: each family has a different rhythm of living and will want to use these activities at different times and in different ways. Perhaps some families will prefer to set aside a particular day and time of the week as their worship time, for instance, Sunday evenings or Wednesday dinner. If you use the weekly format, you might want to use several of the suggestions under **Living Our Worship** at different times during the week. In this way, your worship experience would be extended over several days. Again, the **Remembrances** suggestions could be used at a different time or on a different day than the rest of the worship resources.

Some families might want to divide up the worship activities so that they have a worship segment or way to implement worship for each day of the week. You could begin on Sunday evening with **Preparation** and use the four elements of worship on each of the first four week days. Friday could be **Remembrances** day, and on Saturday, the family might select one of the suggestions from **Living Our Worship** section.

Some families may want to choose only the special days that relate specifically to their family and use the worship actitivies on those days. You may want to save the others so that as the appropriate time comes in your family, you will have the worship resources to guide you. Also, families might use the resources very spontaneously, as they see fit and as the impulse hits the family to worship God around a particular event or happening.

Again, may we stress that these pages are part of our own struggle and journey into understanding who and whose we are. We do not see anything here that is perfect or necessary. These are only ideas. We hope they will work as the raw material for your own family's discovery of worship together. If anything here triggers a better or more complete thought in your mind, go with it. Use your own creations for your worship experiences. By all means adapt, rearrange, or reject these materials as they best suit your family's needs and preferences. And, by all means, experiment and *enjoy* your worship time together. We hope these pages are just the beginning of an exciting adventure for your family. Where that adventure ends, only you and God can determine.

Paul and Hal

I. OUR FAMILY

FAMILY LOVE

Preparation

Beloved, let us love one another; for love is of God, and he who loves is born of God and knows God.

—1 John 4:7

To love is truly to live. We cannot survive without love, and children learn how to love from their families. Love is the deepest and yet simplest emotion we have. The purpose of this worship resource is to guide gently our understanding of love for our family and of how that love can be expressed as love for everyone. Since the child's first experiences of love occur in the context of a family, we need to lift up and celebrate our family love. We must always remember, however, that the basis of our family love is God's love for us.

Worship

Adoration: Praising God

Parent: Praise God for *(name of a family member).*

All: Everyone is important and loved by our family.

Parent: Repeat the phrase above and use another family member's name. After each person's name, have everyone read the response. Continue until you have thanked God for all the members of your family.

Confession: Understanding Us

As a family, pray in silence for the times each of you has not been loving toward one another. Have each member of the family think about these times in silence and ask God to forgive her or him. Conclude your silent prayer by all joining hands and saying together, "We're sorry, God. We love you and each other very much. Amen."

Affirmation: Growing in Faith

Invite a family member to read the story of Jesus raising Lazarus from the dead (John 11:32-44). After reading the story, talk as a family about how Jesus expressed his love for Lazarus in the story. For instance, Jesus spoke to Lazarus, he cried, he touched him, he hugged him, he kissed him. As a family, talk about how you can express your love for one another in these same ways.

Dedication: Living New Life

Ask an older child or teenager to read First Corinthians 13. Read the passage slowly and carefully and ask each of the members of the family to reflect silently on how she or he might live out this beautiful expression of love.

Living Our Worship

Choose one or more of the following:

Design a symbol or a picture to depict your family's love for one another. You might think about a shape (perhaps a circle or a heart) or use a series of phrases or words to symbolize your family's love. Put the symbol in the center of your dining table and hold hands with members of your family as you talk about your family's symbol.

Demonstrate your family's love for one another by talking about events that happened in the past to older members of your family. Tell your children about their grandparents (and even share stories of their great-grandparents, if you knew them). Have an evening of sharing in front of the fireplace or around the kitchen table (you might even want to pop corn and have a party).

Get out the old photo albums and show the children pictures of family members you don't see very often or pictures of your family members when they were younger. Talk about the fun events connected with the pictures and your memories of times with your family.

Make a family tree. Let all the members of your family research the family Bible or talk to older family members to find dates of birth and death and full names of deceased family members. Draw your family tree on a large piece of paper and hang it someplace where your family can see it.

Remembrances

Pray together: Thank you, God, for giving us families to love and care for us. We thank you for *(name a family member)* who loves us by *(name some loving actions or duties he or she performs)*. Continue to insert the name of each member of your family until you have prayed for all of them. Then continue to pray:

"Help us, O God, to show our love for each member of our family as we learn truly to love everyone. Amen."

HOME AND FAMILY

Preparation

Every one then who hears these words of mine and does them will be like a wise man who built his house upon the rock.

—Matthew 7:24

Your home is the place where your family has the opportunity to grow in the love and knowledge of Jesus of Nazareth. Within our families we learn what it means to love and be loved, to respect and be respected, to trust and be trusted.

Worship

Adoration: Praising God

Read or sing together the hymn, "God of Our Life," by Hugh T. Kerr.

God of our life, through all the circling years, We trust in thee;
In all the past, through all our hopes and fears, Thy hand we see.
With each new day, when morning lifts the veil,
We own Thy mercies, Lord, which never fail.

God of the past, our times are in Thy hand; With us abide.
Lead us by faith to hope's true Promised Land; Be Thou our Guide.
With Thee to bless, the darkness shines as light,
And faith's fair vision changes into sight.

God of the coming years, through paths unknown We follow Thee;
When we are strong, Lord, leave us not alone; Our Refuge be.
Be Thou for us in life our Daily Bread,
Our heart's true Home when all our years have sped.

Confession: Understanding Us

Adult: We know that our home should be a place where we show each other a daily example of your Son and our Lord.

All: Forgive us when we do not allow one another to love and be loved because of our unwillingness to trust, forgive, respect, and accept one another.

Child: Lord, help us to have the mind of Jesus so that your Son's love will be shared daily in our home with those we love.

Affirmation: Growing in Faith

Ask a member to read Acts 7:48-49. Then invite each member to share one way in which home provides a place to grow in understanding of Jesus' messages of trust, forgiveness, respect, and acceptance.

Dedication: Living New Life

Pray together the Lord's Prayer. Before you pray, emphasize that your focus is on "thy will be done." We are all involved in doing God's will on earth.

Living Our Worship

Choose one or more of the following:

Ask each member to complete the sentence, "I am acting like Jesus when I ____________________," on a 3 x 5 card. Ask all the family members to carry their cards in their lunch boxes, wallets, purses, school notebooks, or daily calendars, where they will see them during the day as reminders of who they are and to whom they belong.

Take a family picture and place it on the refrigerator or in another central place where the entire family will see it. Under the picture write, "We are doing God's will."

Your family might enjoy making a plaque for the home by using a small piece of wood and some alphabet cereal or macaroni. Glue your message on the board with macaroni and shellac the results.

Remembrances

Read Psalm 127:1: "If the Lord does not build the house, the work of the builders is useless" (TEV).

FAMILY VACATION

Preparation

Where you go I will go.

—Ruth 1:16

A family vacation represents an important investment of time and money by a family. Whether expensive and exotic or a weekend at grandmother's, a vacation is a family event shared by the entire family *together.*

The family's traveling and staying together for a relatively long period of time may invite tension and explosive feelings. Try to relax and remember that family vacations can be among the best memories your family will share. Don't plan to do too much or to see everything in an area. Don't spend too much money so that anyone feels guilty or has to suffer to pay off the bills.

The less expensive and simpler a vacation is, the greater the potential for family happiness, real family communion, and family growth.

Worship

Adoration: Praising God

Pray together, "Our Creator, you gave us this time together and the necessary money to take a vacation. Help us to enjoy the vacation and to enjoy one another. Allow us to see and enjoy new vistas. Allow us to see and enjoy one another in new ways. Amen."

Confession: Understanding Us

Invite family members to think about what this vacation means to them and what they hope to get out of it. Use each moment of silence as a special prayer for God's guidance in having the best possible family vacation. After a few moments of silence, read Psalm 132:14 and then pronounce, "Amen."

Affirmation: Growing in Faith

Provide family members with statements that fit the appropriate part they play in the family vacation. Each statement may be used by one or more members and may be repeated to allow each member to list all of his or her roles:

I am driving my family on this vacation. May I drive safely.

I am riding in the car with my family on this vacation. May I be a good rider and help the driver.

I am going to see many new sights on my vacation. May I look with interest on them.

I am going to meet new people on my vacation. May I be kind and loving toward them.

I am going to new places on my vacation. May I be eager to go.

I am going to fly in an airplane on my vacation. May I be a good passenger and enjoy the flight.

I am going to share motel rooms with other people. May I keep quiet and sleep each night.

I am going to enjoy my vacation. May I have fun.

Dedication: Living New Life

Ask each family member to make a promise to the others about how he or she will behave on vacation. The promise might be to drive carefully, to sleep at night or in the car, to try not to cry, or to try not to get angry. After everyone has made a promise, conclude by saying: "We hope to keep these promises. Help us, God, to keep them. Amen."

Living Our Worship

Assign appropriate tasks to different members to help the family recall their vacation. Ask one member to keep a log or journal on what happened and what was seen. Ask another to record the mileage each day and where you ate; another to record what each picture is and when it is taken, so you can identify your snapshots.

Allow the family members to take turns deciding where you will eat your next meal or what type of food you will have. Keep in mind your time commitments and budget in planning acceptable alternatives for the younger children.

Invite family members, in turn, to entertain the others during travel periods. Plan ahead what you want to do. You might sing, lead games, play charades. Little children will have no trouble coming up with ideas to amuse and entertain.

Remembrances

Plan a family night of sharing about your vacation. Invite some close friends or other family members to join you and tell them all about your vacation. Show your slides and pictures. Make sure each child has an opportunity to tell what he or she remembers.

These moments of sharing with one another and with friends and family will help keep the vacation alive long after it is over. Share all the happy events, all the disappointments, and, most of all, all the funny things that happened. By sharing funny events, you build up a collection of personal anecdotes that are remembrances of your family life together. No one else has the same experiences as your family, so look back upon the past events of the family vacation often and laugh together about them.

YOUTH'S BIRTHDAY

Preparation

Let no one despise your youth, but set the believers an example in speech and conduct, in love, in faith, in purity.

—1 Timothy 4:12

Because birthdays make young people another year older and thus more capable of having adult freedoms and responsibilities, they are exciting and special days for youngsters. It is important that parents remember this need for freedom, this need for focusing on themselves, especially youths' "over against" attitudes that often develop as they seek their own identity and establish their own standards.

Certainly none of us likes being an opponent, but we can accept a youth's challenging and questioning as a normal part of the maturing process. This birthday celebration can be an opportunity to examine values and rules and to celebrate changes and growth in our young people.

Worship

Adoration: Praising God

Gather as a family to celebrate the birthday or the special day honoring your youth. Members may write a litany based on the good things that your son or daughter accomplished in the last year. Begin by thanking God for *(name)*, then ask everyone to join in the response to each good accomplishment with, "Thank you, God, for what *(name)* has done."

Confession: Understanding Us

Ask the person who is honored to read Luke 2:41-52. Discuss as a family what it meant for Jesus to answer his mother in such a way. Ask the youth to describe how Jesus might have felt at that moment in the temple and ask each parent what the parents of Jesus might have felt when Jesus answered them. How does this story of the boy Jesus relate to your family and some of the misunderstandings that occur in your home? Conclude with a prayer: "We thank you for our family and for *(name)*. Help us to understand one another and to show our love and care for one another. You showed us how to love and told us to 'go and do likewise.' Help us to communicate our love more fully. Amen."

Affirmation: Growing in Faith

As a family, review the past year. Ask someone to share a funny story about events in the youth's life in the last year. Ask others to share moments when they felt especially loved by the young person. Thank the youth for these events and conclude by inviting him or her to share personal stories about what has happened in the last year.

Dedication: Living New Life

Gather as a family around the youth in a circle of love while you sing "Happy Birthday" or "Jolly Good Fellow" to him or her. Conclude by shouting in unison, "We love you!"

Living Our Worship

Choose one or more of the following:

Make a covenant with your young person. Ask him or her to identify what he or she would like to do in exchange for additional freedoms. As a family, agree on additional responsibilities and new freedoms. Sign the covenant and ask God to bless the covenant. Put the covenant away where you can find it again.

Ask the members to write love notes to the youth and put these away to be mailed to the youth at a later time. Or hide the notes in the dresser drawer or under the pillow or dinner plate, one every three or six months during the coming year. Mark your calendar so that you remember to do this.

Give your youth a gift of time. Let him or her decide how other members will use their time with him or her. Your youth might choose to use the gifts of time from all the members of the family at once, or individually with each member of the family.

Write your youth a letter in which you describe your feelings of pride. Try to be specific in your listing of your feelings and why you feel this way.

Remembrances

Surprise your youth with the special gift of a scrapbook or photo album full of pictures of him or her. Include drawings to symbolize activities, special awards or recognition, and pictures as a baby and as a child. You might want to make a special recognition award for your youth. Invite all the members to work on the award or scrapbook.

MOTHER'S BIRTHDAY

Preparation

Honor. . . your mother.

—Matthew 15:4

Both the Old and New Testaments speaks of honoring father and mother. At least six references in the Bible pertain to this esteem for one's parents. Matthew, Mark, and Luke all have Jesus repeating, "Honor your father and mother." After all, what could be more appropriate than to show gratitude to the persons who brought us into this world and who have nurtured us in Christian faith?

Yet, our parents include those who live beyond the walls of the home into which we were born. Jesus said: " 'Who are my mother and my brothers?' And looking around on those who sat about him, he said, 'Here are my mother and my brothers! Whoever does the will of God is my brother, and sister, and mother' " (Mark 3:33-35).

Worship

Adoration: Praising God

Read aloud Luke 18:18-30. After your family has had an opportunity to think about the scripture, discuss among yourselves the meaning of giving to others you say you love.

Confession: Understanding Us

Discuss as a family how difficult it is to live out the idea of giving. Is it more blessed to give than to receive? Why do we enjoy receiving gifts more than giving them? What could make it easier than to practice the principle of giving? Raise these questions and others that may come to mind. Then offer a prayer for help in living as a giver of gifts.

Affirmation: Growing in Faith

Share the gifts of love that Mom has given you during the past year of your life together. Be sure not to overlook the day-to-day items you often take for granted. Then form a circle around Mom, placing her in the middle, while the rest of the family holds hands and sings, "For She's a Jolly Good Mother."

Dedication: Living New Life

Take time to decide individually what new responsibilities you might take upon yourself. There are always things that we can do for ourselves that we allow others to do for us. Tell Mom what you will do as your gift to her during the year.

Living Our Worship

Choose one or more of the following:

Plan a special party. (If mother works outside the home, this may have to be done well in advance.) What could possibly be a more appropriate way to honor your mother? Let the entire family help in making the plans. Invite special friends that would make the occasion a joyous one for Mom. Make the decorations for the party items which represent mother's special interests: tickets to the theater, needlecraft items, charcoals and a sketch pad, new paperbacks, or whatever would suit your Mom.

Plan a surprise night out for Mom, perhaps dinner and a movie of her choice. Let Mom decide the details.

Ask each member to write down fond thoughts of Mom and frame them for hanging.

Remembrances

Compose a family prayer for Mom that tells her how special she is to each member of the family.

FATHER'S BIRTHDAY

Preparation

Honor your father.

—*Ephesians 6:2*

As we reach adulthood and beyond, we tend to forget the excitement and joy and sense of accomplishment connected with birthdays. Usually, we try to ignore the day and pretend that we are not any older. For the family, however, and especially for the children, Dad's birthday is a day of great celebration. By celebrating Dad's birthday, we remind him how very important he is to each of the family members. Even if Dad doesn't want to celebrate another year of life, make the day one of celebration for his role as father and in appreciation for all that Dad has done with the family during the past twelve months.

Worship

Adoration: Praising God

Dad: Thank you, God, for this birthday. You gave me another year of life.

Mother: For the love and concern that was expressed toward us this past year, we thank you, God.

First Child: For the happiness and sadness, for the successes and failures of this past year, we thank you, God.

Second Child: For Dad's constant love and caring for each of us, we thank you, God.

All: Amen.

Confession: Understanding Us

Dad: Father in heaven, who taught us how to be fathers through the gift of your son, Jesus, you know me better than I know myself. You have given me this family—my wife, my child (or children), and this opportunity to be a father to them. For the past year you have helped me to love each of them, to be a friend to them, to guide and direct them. For these opportunities, I thank you. For another year of life and health and learning about how to be a father, I thank you. Amen.

Affirmation: Growing in Faith

Gather around Dad in order that each member can give Dad a verbal birthday gift: a compliment or a reminder of something he did during the past year for that member.

Conclude by having an older child read First John 3:1-3.

Dedication: Living New Life

Mother and Children: Father, God, we thank you for our father and for his love and concern for us. We celebrate who he is and what he has given to each of us during the past year as we celebrate his day. Amen.

Living Our Worship

Choose one or more of the following:

Make posters for Dad and place them around the house where he will be sure to see them. Place these in areas where he is often at work. The posters can describe some good quality he has or recall a favorite expression or saying he uses.

Ask each member to make a card for Dad. On the outside of the card, use a drawing of what Dad looks like, and on the inside, the gift of a promise—to share a favorite storybook or to help him clean up his work bench or to do his chores for a week.

Plan a party for Dad. Invite several of his friends and let the children help to plan the party. If the children are younger, they can do their part by going to bed willingly and happily. If they are older, they could help prepare and serve the refreshments to the guests.

Remembrances

On this special day, include all the children, even the youngest, in the planning and buying, wrapping and presenting of gifts. Perhaps each child could make a small gift to present to Dad. The gift need not be expensive—razor blades or needed toilet articles are great. The object here is that even the youngest child participate.

CHILDREN'S DAY

Preparation

Jesus said, "Let the children come to me, and do not hinder them; for to such belongs the kingdom of heaven."

—Matthew 19:14

Jesus loved little children and took time out to be with them. He valued them as full and equal creations of God. This celebration gives us the opportunity to tell our children that we love them and value them, each one, as unique.

The day also gives us the chance to give our children something of ourselves—our time, our skills, our love, and our knowledge. You may wish to avoid purchasing any gifts and, instead, plan a day of fun as a family.

Worship

Adoration: Praising God

Ask a family member to read Matthew 19:13-15. Discuss how Jesus loved the children and why he took time out for the children. Close this discussion with the simple sentence prayer, "We thank you, God, for showing us how to love children with the example your Son, Jesus, gave us. Amen."

Confession: Understanding Us

Parent: God gave us children—
Children: To teach us to dream.
Parent: God gave us the sun—
Children: In which to run and play.
Parent: God gave us grass—
Children: On which to run in bare feet.
Parent: God gave us little girls—
Children: To give us hope for the future.
Parent: God gave us little boys—

Children: To show us visions of what can be.
Parent: God gave us children—
Children: To teach us about patience and love.
All: For making us a family and teaching us to love, we thank you, God.

Affirmation: Growing in Faith

Assign a parent to read Matthew 18:1-5.

Invite each child to take a turn standing in the middle of the room while all the other family members tell the child what is special and unique about him or her. Describe the special events surrounding the child's birth. Help each child understand that he or she is truly lovable during this ceremony.

Celebrate your insights about each child by concluding each child's sharing time with the prayer, "Thank you, God, for giving us *(child's name).* Amen."

Dedication: Living New Life

As a family, use the following prayer: "Thank you, great and wonderful God, for creating children and letting us learn from them. We hope always to see each of our children as separate and unique and loved by you and us. Teach us how to learn from our children. Amen."

Living Our Worship

Choose one or more of the following:

Fix breakfast in bed for your children. Allow them to read or play with favorite toys while you prepare breakfast. They may decide they'd like breakfast in *your* bed with the whole family. For one day a year, ignore the crumbs and enjoy!

Plan a children's day by packing a picnic lunch and doing whatever the children want to do. Let them plan both the menu and the events of the day.

Write your children a love note on the mirror in their rooms. (Use a grease pencil or eyebrow pencil.)

Plan a family celebration: a trip to the park, the zoo, or an amusement park.

Give each child a reprieve from his or her household duties for a few days. Let Mom and Dad do the child's chores.

Remembrances

After the children have prepared for bed, ask them how they liked being special today. Ask them to tell you what was the happiest moment of the day and what, if anything, was sad during their day. Important clues are gained by reflecting on the happiest and saddest moments at a time when we are quiet and ready for bed.

You may want to ask each child what he or she would like you to do to "remember" that she or he is unique and special every day. Negotiate an acceptable "remembrance" and then endeavor to follow the suggestion each day.

MOTHER'S DAY

Preparation

Here are my mother and my brothers! Whoever does the will of God is my brother, and sister, and mother.

—*Mark 3:34-35*

Mother's Day is an excellent opportunity to remember all the persons, including your mother, who have nurtured you in the love and knowledge of Jesus of Nazareth. The rituals of baptism and of dedication often include a statement that carries this thought: Remember the words of the Lord Jesus Christ when he said, "Let the children come to me, and do not hinder them; for to such belongs the kingdom of heaven."

Parents love and care for their children. When children are dedicated or baptized, their parents make promises to God in answering such questions as these:

Do you therefore accept as your duty and privilege to live before this child a life that becomes the gospel and to exercise all godly care that the child be brought up in the Christian faith, be taught the holy scriptures, and learn to give reverent attendance upon the private and public worship of God?

Will you endeavor to keep this child under the ministry and guidance of the church until this child, by the power of God, shall accept the gift of salvation and be confirmed as a full and responsible member of Christ's holy church?

Mother's Day is an appropriate time to return thanks to God for mothers and fathers as the guardians of a child's life with Christ. Mothers have surrounded us with love and faith.

Worship

Adoration: Praising God

Children: Happy Mother's Day, Mom!

Mother: Thanks, *(names of children).*

Father: Hey, what about me?

Children: You can thank God for Mom.

Father: Let us pray. God, we thank you this day for my wife who has mothered us all according to our individual needs. She has given us her best, Lord, with your constant and abiding help. May she always know that we love and care for her as much as she loves and cares for each of us. Amen.

Confession: Understanding Us

Pray in unison: "O Lord, we know that you taught us to love one another. Help us always to remember how you took time for those persons around you who had need of love and compassion. Help us to be ready for the interruptions in our daily lives from those who love us. Help us to listen to them and assure us that, with your help, we can deal with the problem of the moment. Amen."

Affirmation: Growing in Faith

As a family, discuss how you have learned about the love of God through the love of your mother. Discuss how she has offered you her best and spent time with you, in spite of all the other activities in her daily life.

Dedication: Living New Life

Ask one member to read Ephesians 6:1-4.

Following the reading, discuss what the message means in terms of your mother. Discuss the ways she has tried to show you love through discipline and instruction during the past year. One reminder for your discussion: Often what you want is not what is needed to help you to grow in the love and knowledge of Jesus Christ.

Living Our Worship

Choose one or more of the following:

As a family, treat Mom to a homemade supper at home. Let Dad take the lead in organizing and planning the dinner, with the children helping. In homes where mother does most of the cooking, it is important that Dad and the children know how much work goes into preparing the good meals we enjoy.

Take Mom out for dinner at a place she chooses. You may want to order a nice corsage for Mom.

Buy or make a nice greeting card for Mom and invite each member to write a special note to your favorite lady. Thank her for her constant and abiding love shown to each of you during the year.

Remembrances

Make a "This Is Your Life" display for Mom with a picture of each member of the family and with Mom's picture in the middle. Under the pictures you might consider placing a saying that could read, "To Mom, who has taught us how to love one another! Thanks be to God!" You can purchase an 8½ x 11 inch frame with a mat pad cut for smaller photos that depict family members in casual poses.

FATHER'S DAY

Preparation

God so loved the world that he gave his only Son.

—John 3:16

God showed us what it meant to be a good parent when he gave us his Son, Jesus. What it really means to be a parent is seen in our relationship to God: in spite of how many times we fail him or how often we are wrong, God still forgives us and still loves us.

We celebrate the love expressed between God and Jesus, between God and each one of us, and between our own fathers and ourselves.

Worship

Adoration: Praising God

Ask each family member to finish the following prayer: "O God, I thank you for my father because. . . ." Then pray together, "Our Father who art in heaven, you have taught us what it means to have the love of a father. For the example of a father's love, we thank you. Amen."

Confession: Understanding Us

Ask mother to read Luke 11:11-13. Ask father to use the following prayer: "Dear God, I thank you for my family. I thank you that you have made me a father. I am a father by the acts of love that I perform for my wife and children. There are times when I fail. There are times when I am impatient, tired, angry, and frustrated. I have made promises to my family and failed to keep them. I have needed to ask them for forgiveness at times. But because of your model of what it means to be a father, I can keep trying, and I can know that each member of my family loves me, even when I fail. Amen."

Affirmation: Growing in Faith

Gather around father and invite the members to describe how they have experienced father's love in the past. Don't worry about taking turns; just shout out your replies when you think of them.

Dedication: Living New Life

Ask the family members to go up to Dad, one by one, to kiss him, and to tell him that they love him. After all have done this, let all the members of the family say, "Thank you, God, for our father."

Living Our Worship

Choose one or more of the following:

Write Dad a letter telling him how much you love him and hide it where only he can find it.

Organize the children to help prepare a special meal for Dad, with all his favorite foods included.

Give Dad a special present of your time or talents. Write Dad a coupon good for "one hour of silence" or "one free car wash" or "one hour's extra sleep on Saturday morning" or "one week of taking the garbage out."

Arrange to have a portrait of Mom and the children taken by a commercial studio or a friend. You may want to write "We love you" across the bottom of the picture.

Remembrances

Just before the children go to bed, ask them to invite Dad to come to their rooms one by one. Then, as Dad sits on the edge of the bed, suggest that each child tell Dad why he or she loves Dad.

GRADUATION DAY

Preparation

If you continue in my word, you are truly my disciples, and you will know the truth, and the truth will make you free.

—John 8:31-32

Graduation is a time of mixed emotions for both youth and adults, for it evokes memories of the past and hopes and dreams for the future. It is a happy time, clouded by the fact that—for the high school graduate—it is ofen a time to break away from the security of being part of that beloved daily fellowship called family.

No one really knows what the future holds, but it is crucial that we know who holds our future. Therefore, the most religious question that can be posed by the graduate is not *What* am I going to be? but *Who* am I going to be?

Worship

Adoration: Praising God

Ask the graduate to read Hebrews 12:1-2. Follow the reading with a discussion of how God, through the example of Jesus Christ, grants us the wisdom to face the crossroads of our lives.

Confession: Understanding Us

Father: God, help us to listen to your teachings from the scripture.

Mother: Help us to feel the need to share our thoughts with one another as we strive to grow by faith.

Youth: Help us to be grateful for those persons in our lives who teach us the importance of learning. Through learning, we grow with Christ as the head of our lives.

All: Help us to grow and then go into the world and tell the good news of the gospel to all people.

Affirmation: Growing in Faith

As a family, use this meditation: "We believe that the stirrings to be good and faithful servants of Jesus Christ are within each of us. We believe that though we know not what the future holds for us, we know who holds our future."

Dedication: Living New Life

As a family, decide the key learnings that have taken place in your home that enable your family to move into the future together with faith instead of fear. List your confusions and make them your family's diploma to discipleship.

Living Our Worship

Choose one or more of the following:

With the help of your graduate, plan a graduation party. Invite his or her special friends, including teachers, pastors, church school teachers, good friends in your congregation, peers, relatives, and employers. Encourage the guest of honor to say a word at some point during the event about the importance of these friends and the contribution they have made in his or her life.

As a family, decide on an appropriate gift that will communicate the family's support and affirmation. The gift might contribute to further educational pursuits that are important to that person.

Hold a celebratory meal for the graduate at which you describe the special learnings about yourself that have arisen out of your relationship with the guest of honor. Tell your graduate how and where you have seen her or him as a disciple of Jesus Christ.

Ask each family member to contribute to a prayer that the graduate can carry as an affirmation of self. Write your individual thoughts about your graduate's talents that are gifts from God. Add "Thanks be to God." Sign your name.

Remembrances

Allow Dad to read Mark 16:15. Discuss this familiar passage of scripture in terms of your personal understanding of how each member of the family carries a responsibility to share the good news. End with the prayer, "God, help us to go into your kingdom and to be your disciples always. Amen."

PARENTS' WEDDING ANNIVERSARY

Preparation

Tell those who are invited, Behold, I have made ready my dinner, ...come to the marriage feast.

—Matthew 22:4

Holy matrimony "is an honorable estate, instituted of God, and signifying unto us the mystical union which exists between Christ and his church; which holy estate Christ adorned and beautified with his presence in Cana of Galilee."* Because children are a product of our love for each other as husband and wife, it is important that our children are included in the celebration of our wedding anniversary.

Worship

Adoration: Praising God

Husband and wife can share with each other and the children ways in which they have honored each other during the past year. Invite the children to discuss the ways in which they have tried to honor their parents also. Conclude your conversation with special thanks to your parents for who they are and what they have done for you.

Confession: Understanding Us

Invite the children to pray in unison: "O Lord, we are thankful for our parents and the love they share together as well as with each of us, their children. We know that their faith and love for us is a symbol of the love that you have for all your children. May we realize, O

God, that we are able to know and experience love through our parents because you first loved us. Help us as a family always to strive to demonstrate our love for you through our love for one another in our home. Amen."

Affirmation: Growing in Faith

Ask a child to read John 3:16. Talk together about how parents have nurtured their children with faith, hope, and love, so they might grow in the ways of Jesus of Nazareth.

Dedication: Living New Life

Children: Thank you, God, for the love you have expressed to us through our parents' love for us.

Parents: Thank you, God, for showing us your love through our love for each other.

Children: Continue to teach us how to love, God, by helping us to know our parents' love for us daily.

Parents: Let the love between us grow and expand and deepen as we better understand your love for us, O God.

Living Our Worship

Choose one or more of the following:

Invite your pastor to your home a few days before the anniversary to talk about marriage and family life. Discuss the possibilities of having Mom and Dad remarry as a symbol of reaffirming their love for each other under the guidance of God's ever-present care. This celebration would be just for your family and the children would be the witnesses of love between their parents and God.

Talk to grandparents and aunts and uncles who attended the parents' wedding and share the events of the day and the happy memories with your children. Recall all the good and funny events connected with your wedding day.

Allow the children to collect wedding pictures and newspaper clippings. They may want to arrange these mementos in a collage, in a single picture frame.

Allow the children to plan a special anniversary party for Mom and Dad. The children could plan and prepare the food, if they are old enough. If the children are not old enough to plan a party at home, let them plan a picnic or family day at the zoo to celebrate your anniversary.

Remembrances

Take pictures of the anniversary celebration and frame one for each parent. Place these pictures where they will see them daily. Place on Dad's desk at work or on his dresser at home. Mom's picture might go in her office or on her dresser. Make sure all members of the family are in the picture.

NEW HOME DEDICATION

Preparation

You are the light of the world. A city set on a hill cannot be hid. Nor do men light a lamp and put it under a bushel, but on a stand, and it gives lights to all in the house.

—Matthew 5:14-15

As Christians we believe that the home is the cradle of our faith. Our church family thus becomes an extension of our natural family and unites us with other Christians to celebrate God's love for all persons.

In rituals of baptism or dedication we commend a child to the love and care of the total community and recognize the child as a member of the family of God. Parents of children and youth need to establish their homes with faith that is expressed in both word and example, so that the entire family understands the need for worship in their daily lives.

God's rightful place in our lives is head of our households. As you move into your new home and community, celebrate your life as a family with God in your new dwelling. You will want to give God thanks for all the possibilities that lie ahead of you, not only for your family but for all persons who will enter your home.

We pray that peace will be granted to all who enter your new home with you.

Worship

Adoration: Praising God

Ask Dad to read or sing Henry Ware, Jr.'s hymn, "Happy the Home When God Is There."

Happy the home when God is there,
And love fills every breast;
When one their wish, and one their prayer,
And one their heavenly rest.

Happy the home where Jesus' name
Is sweet to every ear;
Where children early lisp his fame,
And parents hold him dear.

Happy the home where prayer is heard,
And praise is wont to rise;
Where parents love the sacred Word
And all its wisdom prize.

Lord, let us in our homes agree
This blessed peace to gain;
Unite our hearts in love to thee,
And love to all will reign.

Confession: Understanding Us

Ask a member to read Luke 18:8. Then discuss how you intend to practice your faith as a family in your new home. What you say will determine the answer to the question posed in the scripture.

Affirmation: Growing in Faith

As a family, discuss the ways in which each individual member needs love and understanding as he or she makes the adjustment to a new home and a new community. Take time to identify the needs of each family member and then remember the apostle Paul's description of love as gentle.

Dedication: Living New Life

As a family, compose a prayer. Invite each member to thank God for one item for which they are personally thankful. After each person has shared, the rest of the family can reply, "Lord, we give you thanks." After everyone has spoken, close with the Lord's Prayer, emphasizing, "Thy will be done."

Living Our Worship

Choose one or more of the following:

Create a sign for the front door that indicates to all who visit your home that you are a Christian family and that you intend to love your neighbors as yourself. This sign will invite your new neighbors to meet you. Your sign might read, "Shalom, which means peace and love, peace to all who enter here. Hi, neighbor!" You might also want to include the ancient Christian symbol of the fish.

As a family, go to greet your new neighbors on your block. The best way to make new friends is to be one yourself.

As a family, visit special points of interest in your neighborhood in order to become familiar with your new community.

As a family, seek out the church of your choice. Perhaps you will want to call ahead and invite the pastor to become acquainted with your family.

Remembrances

Designate a bulletin board or another place where family members can place 3 x 5 cards with the name of a person, place, or opportunity that they have discovered in your new community that they consider attractive. Make a game out of this effort and see who can identify the largest number in a week's time.

Remember, God is with you wherever you are. You can step forth with faith.

*From the Order for the Service of Marriage from *The Book of Worship* of the United Methodist Church.

II. THE FAITH

GOD IN CREATION

Preparation

Remember also your Creator in the days of your youth.
—Ecclesiastes 12:1

We all learn more about God by studying creation. As we study God's world and see how he has made everything according to divine plan, we come closer to God. Creation shouts for us to celebrate because God created the world and all the things in it out of love for us. The world and nature can be an excellent source for studying how God's love works. Take time to reflect on God's creation and respond by saying, "Thank you, God."

Worship

Adoration: Praising God

Read or sing together the first two verses of "This Is My Father's World," by Maltbie D. Babcock:

This is my Father's world, And to my listening ears
All nature sings, and round me rings The music of the spheres.
This is my Father's world: I rest me in the thought
Of rocks and trees, of skies and seas; His hand the wonders wrought.

This is my Father's world, The birds their carols raise,
The morning light, the lily white, Declare their maker's praise.
This is my Father's world: He shines in all that's fair;
In the rustling grass I hear him pass, He speaks to me everywhere.

Confession: Understanding Us

Have each member of the family who can, read about one day in the story of God's creation in Genesis 1:1-2:3. After each day of creation is read, think as a family about how important that part of creation is to you. Conclude your discussion by saying together, "God saw that it was good."

Affirmation: Growing in Faith

Have someone read Luke 12:22-29. Talk about what it means for God to care for all of creation, even people. Talk about how your family can help to share in God's creation by caring for the world and for creatures.

Dedication: Living New Life

Pray: "Holy God, it is so good that you created a good world and that you care for it. Help us to share in the love and care of your world. Help us to realize how much you love and care for each of us. Amen."

Living Our Worship

Choose one or more of the following:

Plan a family outing. You might want to take a picnic lunch and go to a park or the woods and admire God's creation. Have a special grace before you eat to thank God for the beauty of the world.

Visit the zoo and talk about how and why God created all the animals in the world. You might explore more about the exotic animals and where they live naturally. Try to understand how God's plan works for all these animals.

Ask each member of your family to select his or her favorite picture or painting of creation. Some members of the family might choose to paint or color their own pictures. Share these pictures with your family and thank God for creation.

Collect examples of God's creation. You might have a family outing to a park or even in your backyard. Gather flowers or leaves or nuts or fruits or plants. Arrange the fruits of God's creation in a basket or bowl in the center of your dining table. Let the family talk about the fruits of God's creation before grace at each meal this week.

Remembrances

Sing or read together "For the Beauty of the Earth," by Folliot S. Pierpoint:

For the beauty of the earth, For the glory of the skies,
For the love which from our birth Over and around us lies:
Lord of all, to thee we raise This our hymn of grateful praise.

For the beauty of each hour Of the day and of the night,
Hill and vale, and tree and flower, Sun and moon, and stars of light:
Lord of all, to thee we raise This our hymn of grateful praise.

For the joy of ear and eye, For the heart and mind's delight,

For the mystic harmony Linking sense to sound and sight:
Lord of all, to thee we raise This our hymn of grateful praise.

For the joy of human love, Brother, sister, parent, child,
Friends on earth, and friends above; For all gentle thoughts and mild:
Lord of all, to thee we raise This our hymn of grateful praise.

BAPTISM

Preparation

Turn away from your sins and be baptized.

—*Mark 1:4* (TEV)

Baptism is one of two sacraments in Protestant churches. The ritual of baptism has historically been the rite through which one is initiated into the community of the Christian faith.

Jesus and, most likely, his disciples were baptized by John the Baptist. Following the death of Jesus, the custom seems to have been used much more widely as a symbol of inner cleansing and the mark of new life.

Worship

Adoration: Praising God

Read or sing together the hymn, "Now Thank We All Our God," by Martin Rinkart.

Now Thank we all our God With heart and hands and voices,
Who wondrous things hath done, In whom his world rejoices;
Who, from our mothers' arms, Hath blessed us on our way
With countless gifts of love, And still is ours today.

Confession: Understanding Us

Pray together:

Father God,
Help us to give our lives to you in all we do or say.
Help us to understand that in serving others in need, we serve you.
Help us to strengthen our faith through hardship, disappointment, disillusionment, conflict, frustration, failure, and loss.
Help us to live for you in such a way that our faith might be

contagious enough that someone, somewhere, sometime, might sense your presence. Amen.

Affirmation: Growing in Faith

Have a member of the family read Ephesians 4:1-6. Talk about how each individual family member can show love by being helpful to others and so affirm his or her baptism as one of Christ's children.

Dedication: Living New Life

Have each family member pause for a moment of silent prayer, asking God to help each to listen to his or her conscience for wisdom. Let each family member focus on the meaning of living his or her baptism by helping others.

Following the silent prayer, have the family members each say aloud in turn: "*(person's name)*, remember you are baptized!"

Living Our Worship *Choose one or more of the following:*

Take a family picture and place it on an 8½ x 11 piece of paper. Print these words under your family picture:

> Brothers and sisters of the household of faith, I commend to your love and care these persons whom we this day recognize as members of the family of God. God being my help, *I will try to live that they may grow* in the knowledge and love of God the Father, through our Savior Jesus Christ!*

Place this picture and these words on the family refrigerator or in a spot where the entire family passes on a regular basis.

Using the service of baptism and the service of communion, talk about how they are similar in terms of God calling and persons responding. Your pastor will be happy to let you use a hymnal to look at how baptism is our sacrament of belonging and communion is our sacrament of nurturing that reminds us who we are and to whom we belong!

Remembrances

As a family, sing or say this familiar benediction by John Fawcett as a sending forth for the family into daily life together:

*adapted from the sacrament of Baptism of The United Methodist Church.

Blest be the tie that binds Our hearts in Christian love;
The fellowship of kindred minds Is like to that above.

COMMUNION

Preparation

"I am the bread of life," Jesus told them. "He who comes to me will never be hungry; he who believes in me will never be thirsty. Now, I told you that you have seen me but will not believe. Everyone whom my Father gives me will come to me. I will never turn away anyone who comes to me, because I have come down from heaven to do not my own will but the will of him who sent me."

—John 6:35-38 (TEV)

Communion is a special meal that Protestants consider a sacrament because it is an obligation and an oath of allegiance. Jesus held his Last Supper in an upper room with his disciples as a symbol to all who were gathered with him that "man shall not live by bread alone" (Luke 4:4). Communion is our way of remembering the words of Jesus that we must "worship the Lord your God, and him only shall you serve" (Luke 4:8).

Worship

Adoration: Praising God

Begin your worship by having Dad lead the family in the Lord's Prayer. This is not just a prayer Jesus gave us to say, but our guidelines for daily expression of a life of faithfulness to God. As you say your prayer of faithfulness together, focus on the phrase "give us this day our daily bread."

Confession: Understanding Us

Ask mother to remind the family members that we need to ask God to forgive us our sins, just as we want others to forgive us for the wrongs we do to them.

Ask each member to pray in silence to God for the times when each has been unforgiving toward others. Remember that God always forgives us our sins because he loves us.

Affirmation: Growing in Faith

Ask one child to read Psalm 4 to the rest of the family. Talk about the psalm's emphasis on our relationship with God. Try to cite everyday examples of these in your life.

Dedication: Living New Life

Using yet another phrase of the Lord's Prayer, "thy kingdom come, thy will be done, on earth as it is in heaven," ask each family member to think silently on how she or he can do God's will in your family circle. Think about ways each person can be more patient and kind to one another.

Living Our Worship

Choose one or more of the following:

Discuss the word *communion.* Remember that we are one in Christ, called and committed as Christians to share life at its deepest level with one another. We share through love and patience and by giving of our time, talents, and financial resources.

Ask family members to find direct references in the New Testament to Jesus' breaking bread in the form of a meal. (Use the concordance in the back of your family Bible.)

Remembrances

Ask an older child to read Acts 2:43-47. After this scripture on life among the believers, discuss the importance of praising God in your family.

DEVOTIONAL LIFE

Preparation

In the beginning was the Word, and the Word was with God, and the Word was God.

—John 1:1

In focusing on the devotional life of the family, think of the central place the Bible plays in devotions. Using the Bible with the family invites each person to know God's love and to live in a relationship of love with God and others. The Bible is the story of God's love for us, the basic foundation for faith.

Teaching the Bible begins at home. As our children see that we love and value them as special, they will learn that we treat them just as God treats all of us. Our love is biblical, our response because God first loved us. As the children hear and study the Bible stories, they come to recognize these stories as part of their own faith heritage and a cornerstone for their daily living.

Worship

Adoration: Praising God

Read Psalm 119:1-16 aloud to the family. Discuss what this psalm means when it talks about "walk[ing] in the law of the Lord" and not forgetting "thy word." As a family, discuss what the words *ordinances, precepts,* and *statutes* mean. How do we know God's intention for our lives by reading from the Bible? Talk about the Bible as the "Word of God." Conclude with a prayer thanking God for the Bible and his relationship of love.

Confession: Understanding Us

Read the story of the burning bush and Moses (Exodus 3:1-15) and talk about how God encountered Moses. Try to understand that the confrontation itself is significant, not how it occured. Talk about how God told Moses, "I am who I am." What does this mean about God for your family?

Affirmation: Growing in Faith

Take a large piece of paper and place it in the middle of the dining table. Write the words, "Love is . . .", on the paper and ask all the members to finish the sentence. Cover the paper with sketches illustrating the sentence endings. After you have filled the sheet, hang it on the refrigerator door or a bulletin board and discuss what each of you wrote or drew on the sheet and why. Conclude by reading First Corinthians 13.

Dedication: Living New Life

Read John 3:16 out loud and then discuss what it means. Try to examine the scripture at three levels: What does the passage *say*—words, facts, what happened? What does the passage *mean*—what is the reason for the passage being in the Bible? What is the *message* of the passage for your own family? What difference does reading this passage make for your own decision-making from day to day? Try to come up with a slogan to summarize the passage. Print the slogan on a piece of paper and hang it where you can all see it.

Living Our Worship

Choose one or more of the following:

You might want to purchase a Bible for each member of your family. Encourage each member to read and use the Bible daily.

Select a time of day, perhaps at the children's bedtime or at breakfast or dinner, when the family can gather for daily Bible reading. Your minister or church can furnish suggested readings.

Select a Bible to present to a special friend or relative, perhaps as a birthday or Christmas gift. If your friend is young, choose a children's edition of the Bible, or if elderly, a large-print edition. As you present your gift, tell the receiver how you enjoy reading from the Bible and what your favorite passages are.

Take the slogan your family created and share it with friends or relatives. You may want to make bumper stickers by cutting strips of white contact paper and printing the slogan with magic marker.

Remembrances

Thank God in prayer for the Bible and the heroes and heroines of Bible times. Invite family members to talk about their favorite characters from the Bible—why a character is a favorite and what they remember most about the character. Close your prayer with thanks to God for the persons in today's world who continue to be receptive to the call of God and to live in a faithful way.

PRAYER

Preparation

In praying do not heap up empty phrases as the Gentiles do; for they think that they will be heard for their many words. Do not be like them, for your Father knows what you need before you ask him.

—Matthew 6:7-8

Teaching children to pray is a process that needs to begin at an early age. It is much like swimming lessons. Children can be taught to swim as infants because they are not afraid of water and because they trust their instructor who is wading into the water with them.

A good method for teaching children to pray is to suggest to them that it is like talking with their best friend, sibling, or parent. Prayer is a message that comes from the heart. The intent of the prayer is far more important than the sender's message.

We suggest that you start with short rhythmic prayers and progress to individual feelings and concerns of the children surrounding their life experiences. Also, don't hesitate to pray often in their presence so that they understand that it is something you (their teacher) feel comfortable with yourself.

Remember, and teach your children: God accepts us where we are.

Worship

Adoration: Praising God

Assign an adult member to read Matthew 6:7-15. At the conclusion of your Bible reading, say together the Lord's Prayer.

Confession: Understanding Us

Assign an adult member to remind the family that Jesus not only taught us how to pray but also gave us his prayer as a guide for daily life.

Together as a family, talk about to whom the Lord's Prayer is addressed and what its message means.

Affirmation: Growing in Faith

Have a family discussion with God. To prepare for your prayer, first talk about what it means to be in an attitude of prayer. (A clue: "To love your neighbor as yourself.")

Now you're ready to pray about a family joy or sorrow.

Dedication: Living New Life

Individuals may thank God for one gift or person. Participants can follow this by asking God to forgive something they'd like to change to improve the quality of their life together.

Living Our Worship

Choose one or more of the following:

Allow each member of the family unit to write a prayer to God that expresses thanks for each other member of the family. Then, repeat these prayers individually while the rest of the family listens very carefully to what is being said.

Ask family members to say why God is important to them. Gather these thoughts and put together a family prayer that could be used on a regular basis with the family unit.

Create a new prayer each month. Use each family's individual enthusiasm about the particular month under consideration.

Create a special prayer for each holiday of the year. Ask various family members to take responsibility for gathering information for the prayer from the rest of the family and then lead the prayer at a family gathering.

Remembrances

Write a statement to guide your family in the creative process of developing prayers. Think of the key ingredients that need to go into a prayer: praise, thanksgiving, forgiveness, and so forth. You may want to place your statement on prayer in a place that will be seen by the family on a daily basis.

GIVING

Preparation

God loves a cheerful giver.

—2 Corinthians 9:7

Sometimes we give because we feel we have to give and sometimes we give because we want to give. Some persons have misunderstood why they feel the need to give to God. God does not want us to give because we feel we must, but because we want to give. When we consider all that God has given us, we need to give in response to God's generosity.

Help your children achieve a new understanding of the meaning of giving. Help them understand that we give when we want to give and that we truly give when we give all that we have, not just from our abundance.

Worship

Adoration: Praising God

Sing or read the first verse of "For the Beauty of the Earth," by Folliot S. Pierpoint.

For the beauty of the earth,
For the glory of the skies,
For the love which from our birth
Over and around us lies:

Lord of all, to thee we raise
This our hymn of grateful praise.

Confession: Understanding Us

As a family, talk about the times you have given money, gifts, time, or talent and have not wanted to give. Talk about how repaying something "owed" is not really giving. Conclude your discussion with a prayer asking God for forgiveness and for help in learning how to give appropriately.

Affirmation: Growing in Faith

Ask a member to read Luke 21:1-4 to the rest of the family. Talk about the difference in giving in this story: the widow gave all that she had, while the rich persons gave only out of their abundance. What does it mean to give all that we have?

Dedication: Living New Life

Recall the famous verse, "For God so loved the world that he gave his only Son." Conclude with the prayer, "Thank you, God, for giving all that you had, your only Son, so that we might have an example of what it means truly to give. Help us to learn to give all that we have, not just out of our abundance. Amen."

Living Our Worship

Choose one or more of the following:

Select a short period of time each week, perhaps fifteen minutes early Monday morning, and set this period aside as thanksgiving time. During this time, ask the family members to think about whom they want to thank for some act of kindness during the past week. Family members may want to write notes or tell the person thanks in person. This time can be a new learning experience in how to give to one another.

Select a charity or cause that your family wants to support, either financially or with your time. Agree as a family what each of you will contribute.

Try to reduce the number of gifts you buy for friends and loved ones. Rather than buying a gift, think about what the recipient of your gift might really enjoy. Perhaps you can make a gift or donate money to a charity in this person's name. Consider changing some of your giving habits.

Remembrances

Sing or say the Doxology together:

Praise God, from whom all blessings flow;
Praise him, all creatures here below;
Praise him above, ye heavenly host;
Praise Father, Son, and Holy Ghost.

MISSIONS

Preparation

And the King will answer them, "Truly, I say to you, as you did it to one of the least of these my brethren, you did it to me."

—Matthew 25:40

Every Christian is concerned about worldwide missions, including the development of Third World countries, self-help programs, and preserving the dignity of the persons being assisted.

Even the youngest child is capable of realizing that people are hungry in the world and our commandment from Jesus is to "go and do likewise" in our love and concern for God's world.

Worship

Adoration: Praising God

Ask one member to read John 21:15-17. This story suggests how we are to show our love for Jesus by feeding and clothing others who are in need. Conclude your reading of the scripture by thanking God for the opportunity to share with others.

Confession: Understanding Us

Pray together: "Our Father, we ask your forgiveness for the times when we are slow to accept our responsibility for all of your children. Help us to learn how to say yes to those who need our help and not to refuse those who might be hungry or without clothes and shelter, no matter where they may live. We ask for your patience and thank you for opportunities to share our gifts with others. Amen."

Affirmation: Growing in Faith

Discuss a new family covenant. Decide how to change patterns in your family's lifestyle that are wasteful. Then pledge the money you save to a missions project. Your family might covenant with God to cut down on snacking and desserts or to entertain guests and relatives more simply or to use less meat or to study more about good nutrition and how to use more fresh fruits and vegetables in your family's diet. Once your family has agreed on a covenant, write it down, have everyone sign it, and place it on your refrigerator door or in the center of your dining table.

Dedication: Living New Life

Write a letter to your church about your new covenant and mail a copy to your pastor.

Living Our Worship

Choose one or more of the following:

Study the problem of hunger in the world and what you can do about it. Libraries should have information on the topic. Share your research with your family and with friends.

As a family, select a mission to support. You may choose an interdenominational program or any denominational program of your church. An excellent mission for a family is to adopt a child through a church-related program and support this child each month.

Write to missionaries, expressing interest in and concern for their work. Ask them how your family can help them. Offer your thoughts, your prayers, and other kinds of support. Your church can help you select a missionary to write to.

Raise money for a missions project by saving your change in a special bank. Or eat a simple meal once a week. Or ask each family member to raise enough money to equal twenty cents for each year of his or her age.

Remembrances

Begin your plans to celebrate holidays with inexpensive homemade items. As a family, decide to eliminate gifts to one another and plan to entertain family and guests with simpler and less expensive meals. Plan to share the financial savings with a mission project chosen by your family.

CELEBRATING OUR GIFTS AND DIFFERENCES

Preparation

We have many parts in the one body, and all these parts have different functions. In the same way, though we are many, we are one body in union with Christ, and we are all joined to each other as different parts of one body. So we are to use our different gifts in accordance with the grace that God has given us.

—Romans 12:4-6 (TEV)

Thanks be to God that we are all created as individuals and that we have encounters with persons who are at different levels of development in various areas of life. Each of us has unique skills and talents. We find persons who are gifted and persons who are severely limited.

Because persons have different gifts in life, all persons can learn from one another. As we live in community in the household of faith, we can improve our skills and celebrate our differences. We can affirm our differences as being God-given and a part of God's master plan for his world. Individual differences, though sometimes challenging to live with, enrich and enhance our family life. Discover how each member of your family is different and affirm each of these different gifts from God.

Worship

Adoration: Praising God

As a family, sing the traditional American folk song, "He's Got the Whole World in His Hands."

He's got the whole world in his hands,
He's got the whole wide world in his hands,
He's got the whole world in his hands,
He's got the whole world in his hands.

He's got the wind and rain in his hands,
He's got the wind and rain in his hands,
He's got the wind and rain in his hands,
He's got the whole world in his hands.

He's got the tiny little baby in his hands,
He's got the tiny little baby in his hands,
He's got the tiny little baby in his hands,
He's got the whole world in his hands.

He's got you and me, brother, in his hands,
He's got you and me, sister, in his hands,
He's got everybody in his hands,
He's got the whole world in his hands.

Confession: Understanding Us

Father: Forgive us, Lord, for not listening to one another.
Mother: Forgive us, Lord, for not valuing our differences.
Children: Forgive us, Lord, for not always liking our differences.
All: Lord, each of us is made to be different. Help us to use our different talents in our family. Forgive us, Lord, for not listening to your message that asks us to love others as we love ourselves.

Affirmation: Growing in Faith

Read Matthew 25:14-29 aloud. Discuss Jesus' request that we use the talents we possess if we are to please him. Also discuss how to help others with special talents in such a way that they grow and develop because of your relationship. Jesus went out of his way to help others in life and we need to do the same if we are his children.

Dedication: Living New Life

As a family, think of the gifts each of you possesses. Share these gifts with one another; then read First Corinthians 12:27-31 and 13:1-3. How can love help you share talents with others around you in your daily life?

Living Our Worship

Choose one or more of the following:

Plan to have your family visit a school for persons with learning disabilities of all types. Notice the talents these persons have, despite their handicaps. Also think of the handicaps you have and the many persons who are dedicated to helping you in your journey toward growth and maturity.

Ask each member to pick one specific activity or discipline and to investigate the time and techniques required to improve his or her skill in this area. Then dedicate the family to helping those members who want to improve their skills.

List your talents and those which you would like to use better. Place the list on the refrigerator, on your mirror, or in some other place where you can see it daily. Use this list to remind you to be thankful to God for gifts and for the ability to learn and grow in relationship with others around you.

Remembrances

Read Romans 12:4-8. After discussing how your family members share their talents, conclude with a prayer in which you name each member and his or her individual talents. Your prayer might begin, "Thank you, God, for making each of us special. We thank you for father. His talents are ________________________. We also thank you for mother whose talents are ________________________." Conclude by naming each child and listing his or her talents.

III. FEELINGS

HOPES AND DREAMS

Preparation

He said to them, "Hear this dream which I have dreamed."

—Genesis 37:6

All of us have hopes and dreams. The list of dreamers in the biblical message is long. Jacob; Joseph; Isaiah; John the Baptist; Jesus' mother, Mary—all were dreamers. Much of the dreaming and hoping had to do with the Messiah and the coming of God's kingdom here on earth. How appropriate that we as a family talk about our dreams and hopes and how they might be related to the coming of the Kingdom! We need to help children realize that dreams and hopes can come true and that we can work to achieve our hopes and dreams.

Worship

Adoration: Praising God

Open your worship time by reading or singing "O Come, O Come, Emmanuel."

O come, O come, Emmanuel,
And ransom captive Israel,
That mourns in lonely exile here
Until the Son of God appear.
Rejoice! Rejoice! Emmanuel
Shall come to thee, O Israel!

O come, thou Wisdom from on high,
And order all things, far and nigh;
To us the path of knowledge show,
And cause us in her ways to go.
Rejoice! Rejoice! Emmanuel
Shall come to thee, O Israel!

O come, Desire of nations, bind
All people in one heart and mind;
Bid envy, strife, and quarrels cease;
Fill the whole world with heaven's peace.
Rejoice! Rejoice! Emmanuel
Shall come to thee, O Israel!

O come, thou Day-spring, come and cheer
Our spirits by thine advent here;
Disperse the gloomy clouds of night,
And death's dark shadows put to flight.
Rejoice! Rejoice! Emmanuel
Shall come to thee, O Israel!

Talk about what this hymn says about some of the hopes and dreams for the Messiah.

Confession: Understanding Us

Assign a family member to read Isaiah 2:2-4. Then talk about your own hopes and dreams for a Messiah. Do the images and hopes in this scripture make sense to your family today? Why or why not?

Affirmation: Growing in Faith

Invite each member to share one of his or her hopes or dreams for the future. Listen carefully, trying not to criticize or judge the hope or dream. Talk about each person's dream or hope and how it might be achieved.

Dedication: Living New Life

Write a prayer to conclude your worship time. In the prayer, share your hopes and dreams and what each of you intends to do to achieve that hope. Ask God's blessing on your hopes and dreams and aid in achieving them.

Living Our Worship

Choose one or more of the following:

Why not post your dreams on a piece of paper where you can see them and remember them? Often we can achieve some of our hopes and dreams if we are reminded of them and begin to work on them. Sometimes, this process is long-term, and young children need help in understanding that the fruition of their dreams and hopes may be delayed.

As a family, agree on a dream or hope for which you are all willing to work. Post this dream or hope near your family calendar and establish a schedule of what needs to be accomplished by whom to achieve your goal.

Do some Bible research on some of the great dreamers of the Bible. What were some of their hopes and dreams, and how did they work to accomplish their hopes and dreams? Share your findings with your family.

Remembrances

Read or sing the first verse of the hymn, "O Young and Fearless Prophet," by S. Ralph Harlow.

O young and fearless Prophet of ancient Galilee:
Thy life is still a summons to serve humanity,
To make our thoughts and actions less prone to please the crowd,
To stand with humble courage for truth with hearts uncowed.

You might want to rethink some of your dreams after hearing this hymn.

FEARS OF FAILURE

Preparation

Confess your sins to one another, and pray for one another, that you may be healed.

—James 5:16

Often we are afraid to try something new because we fear that we will fail. We all have these fears of failure, no matter what our age. By talking about our fears, we often find they become less frightening. As we learn to share our fears with those we love, we see that all our emotions, even fears, are an important part of us. By sharing fears, we bring them out in the open and confront them. As we share with our loved ones, we better understand ourselves and others. Our sharing brings us closer to each other and to God.

Worship

Adoration: Praising God

Read Psalm 23 aloud. Study the psalm line by line. Try to understand better how the author of the psalm is reassured by his faith in God. Help even your youngest child to hear the assurance and comfort in the lines of this psalm.

Confession: Understanding Us

Invite each member of the family to finish the following sentences and talk about the answers. Allow each member of the family to express his or her true fears without judgment. Remember, these fears are real to the person who expresses them. Complete the following sentences:

I fear ______________________________.

The reason I fear trying to do _______________ is because __________.

I am afraid I might fail to __________________.

Conclude your sharing by thanking God for special loved ones with whom we can share our fears.

Affirmation: Growing in Faith

Talk about what your family members fear, especially new experiences where they fear they might fail. Try to help each person to realize that he or she can reach out and risk trying something new without being judged by other family members. Talk about how each person can learn new skills or improve his or her talents so that he or she might feel comfortable in trying to do something he or she feared.

Dedication: Living New Life

Read or sing together the hymn, "What a Friend We Have in Jesus" by Joseph M. Scriven.

What a friend we have in Jesus,
All our sins and griefs to bear!
What a privilege to carry
Everything to God in prayer!
O what peace we often forfeit,
O what needless pain we bear,
All because we do not carry
Everything to God in prayer!

Have we trials and temptations?
Is there trouble anywhere?
We should never be discouraged;

Take it to the Lord in prayer.
Can we find a friend so faithful
Who will all our sorrows share?
Jesus knows our every weakness;
Take it to the Lord in prayer.

Are we weak and heavy laden,
Cumbered with a load of care?
Precious Savior, still our refuge:
Take it to the Lord in prayer.
Do thy friends despise, forsake thee?
Take it to the Lord in prayer!
In his arms he'll take and shield thee;
Thou wilt find a solace there.

After you have talked about the song and what the words mean, read the first verse of the song as a concluding prayer.

Living Our Worship

Choose one or more of the following:

Talk about how you have overcome past fears. Ask the adults to share what their childhood fears were and how they risked failure to do things. Try to share honestly and try not to diminish your childhood fears. Allow time for the children to share how they overcame their fears.

Decide to pray each day for the ability to risk trying something new. Pray as a family for the strength to allow your family members to overcome their fear of failure.

Write down your family's fears on a sheet of paper and put the list away in a drawer. Bring out the list in six months and talk about how your own fears have changed or diminished. Ask your family members if their fears have changed or diminished.

Remembrances

Read Exodus 3:1-4, 17. This passage is about Moses' confrontation with God at the burning bush. Discuss what Moses feared and how he overcame his fears. Conclude by thanking God for helping us to overcome our fears that we will fail.

RIVALRY AND JEALOUSY

Preparation

His brothers were jealous of him.

—Genesis 37:11

Since the days of Jacob and his sons—and before—children and youth have been jealous of their brothers and sisters. Often a child's need to feel unique and special is expressed in negative ways toward parents and the other children. We need to continue to reassure each of our children of her or his unique place in our love and to try, as best we can, to give individual attention to each child. Each child also needs to learn how to cope with jealous feelings and to share his or her parents' love and attention with other family members.

Worship

Adoration: Praising God

Parent: Thank you, God, for our oldest *(name)*. He (she) is special to us because ______________________________.

Child: Thank you, God, for our sister / brother *(name)*. He (she) is special to us because______________________________.

(Continue this for each child. Try to identify a special characteristic or skill that makes each child unique.)

Confession: Understanding Us

Hold a family discussion about jealousy and rivalry among the children. Ask each member to describe how he or she feels when instances of rivalry or jealousy occur. Try hard not to deny or criticize anyone's feelings. Each person needs to know that her or his feelings are valid and acceptable. End the conversation by joining hands and asking God to guide each of you in your expressions of love and concern for the others.

Affirmation: Growing in Faith

Ask a member to read the story of the prodigal son, Luke 15:11-32.

Identify the feelings of each of the main characters: the father, the older son, the younger son. Talk about how each felt at various times in the story—when the younger son left home, while he was gone, and when he returned. Talk about the times in your own family when each of you might have experienced some of these feelings. Try to understand how each character really felt.

Dedication: Living New Life

Form a circle of love by placing one child in the center surrounded by other family members. Join hands to enclose this child and then pray. Ask God to help each of you recognize every member is unique. Ask God to help you find ways to give undivided time and attention to this special child. Offer this same prayer for each child.

Living Our Worship

Choose one or more of the following:

Ask each member to list ten qualities or characteristics for each child in the family. An older brother or sister or parent will need to help a young child write the list. Do not share this list with anyone but the person about whom you are writing.

Set aside a special day for each child. Name this day *(child's name)'s* Day and post the child's name and picture on the family's breakfast table. Allow the special child to select the menu for the meals that day and to plan how the leisure time for that day will be spent.

Invite each member to choose what he or she would like the family to do as a unit and to plan these activities. Let the person who selected the activity plan the event and be in charge.

Invite each child to write his or her name in the family calendar or datebook. Set aside one hour—at least—for each child and make a date for Mom and Dad with that child. You will need to make other arrangements for child care for the other children in the family. Plan a special activity for your time together.

Remembrances

During a moment of quiet in your family—perhaps at bedtime—go to each child and spend a few minutes alone with him or her. Talk to each child about what she or he means to you and end with a hug and a kiss. Encourage brothers and sisters to have these same quiet, private conversations with their siblings.

ANGER

Preparation

A fool gives full vent to his anger, but a wise man quietly holds it back.

—Proverbs 29:11

Anger is a part of each of our lives. It is an emotion, a real and necessary human feeling. Most of us are concerned and ill at ease when someone expresses anger, especially when the anger is addressed to us. But anger is an honest and rational reaction to what happens to us at times.

Anger helps us to express ourselves, but ways we choose to express our anger can be destructive. We need to help all the family members express their anger in helpful and meaningful ways. To deny or suppress our anger is not helpful to family life, but the expression of our anger needs to be appropriate and useful. Anger, properly expressed, can lead to problem solving and better understanding and intimacy in our family.

Worship

Adoration: Praising God

Ask a family member to read Ephesians 4:26 and discuss the scripture. Help the children realize that anger is a normal and natural response to certain situations. Identify what makes you angry. Concentrate on the part of the scripture lesson that stresses *not* staying angry all day.

Confession: Understanding Us

Think about times when you have seen people express their anger in an inappropriate way.

Conclude by reading Matthew 5:23-24. Recognize that Jesus stressed the need for quick resolutions to our anger and appropriate behaviors toward those who have made us angry.

Affirmation: Growing in Faith

In Ephesians 4:15, Paul talks about "speaking the truth in love." We must learn to express our anger in ways that do not harm our love relationships. As a family practice, send "I-messages" rather than "You-messages." An "I-message" lets our feelings be expressed without judging or condemning another person. "You-messages" are often put-downs, insults, and accusations.

Dedication: Living New Life

Conclude this celebration by remembering the Christian dimension of anger—forgiveness. Read Matthew 6:14 and pray together as a family for greater forgiveness and acceptance of one another.

Living Our Worship

Choose one or more of the following:

As a family, continue to practice sending "I-messages" which concentrate on how *you* feel. Try to continue this form of communication until each of you feels less defensive and freer to express more of his or her angry feelings.

As a family, discuss how you might work out your anger physically. You may want to set up a punching bag in the basement or put several old pillows in a corner of the basement for family members to use when angry.

Find a small box to call your family's anger box. Try practicing placing your angry feelings into the box and taking out good feelings. Either pretend to put the feeling in or write out your reason for being angry and put the slip of paper in the box.

Remembrances

Jesus refused to play judge in a family argument. Read Luke 12:13-14. Jesus concentrated on the question of what can be done now rather than on who was right or wrong. Often you cannot change events that make you angry, but you can share your feelings in a helpful way and work toward love and forgiveness within your family.

GUILT AND TRUST

Preparation

Your guilt is taken away, and your sin forgiven.

—Isaiah 6:7

Guilt and an inability to trust are real, and we all have experienced these emotions, no matter how young we are. Often our guilt comes from something we have done for which we feel ashamed, and we are afraid to trust other persons or God enough to ask for forgiveness. In this worship service, we will explore how guilt is often related to our lack of trust. If only we can trust God and others to forgive us, our guilt can be removed.

Worship

Adoration: Praising God

Ask one member of the family to read Psalm 37:1-9. Talk as a family about what these verses say about trusting in God and trying to live a life free of guilt in God's sight. Try to talk about specific ways you can show your trust in God as a family.

Confession: Understanding Us

Have a silent prayer in which each of you think about something you did that caused you to feel guilty. Try to think about one specific thing you did and how you felt. You do not need to share this memory aloud, unless you want to. (If anyone does share, don't act shocked or judge the person. Listen in love and forgiveness.)

Affirmation: Growing in Faith

Ask a family member to read Romans 3:23-24 aloud. Talk about what these brief verses tell us about guilt and trusting in God. Notice that *everyone* has sinned and felt guilty and that God has forgiven our sin and our guilt when we have asked his forgiveness.

Dedication: Living New Life

Pray together, "Thank you, God, for removing our guilt and for forgiving us of our sins. We know that we can trust in your love and forgiveness. Help us to trust and obey, for there's no other way to be happy in Jesus, but to trust and obey. Amen."

Living Our Worship

Choose one or more of the following:

Make a chart for your wall or refrigerator. Write the title "Forgiveness Chart" on the top of a page and then the words "I Need Forgiveness" on the left side of the page and the words "You are Forgiven" on the right side of the page. Any family member who feels guilty can sign his or her name on the left side. Any family member who wishes to forgive someone can sign his or her name on the right side of the page.

Make a "Guilt Jar" for your dining table. Fill a jar with slips of paper that read "You are forgiven" and place the jar in the middle of the table. Let various family members remove a slip from the jar whenever they feel guilty.

Read Luke 18:9-14 about the Pharisee and the tax collector. As a family, discuss how you need to prepare yourselves for asking for God's forgiveness. What attitude is important? How can you achieve this attitude?

Remembrances

As a family, write a prayer asking God to help each of you to learn how to ask for forgiveness from each other and how each of you can learn to offer forgiveness to each other. Thank God that he taught us how to remove guilt from each other by forgiving one another when we ask for forgiveness.

IV. CHANGE IN OUR LIVES

CHANGE

Preparation

Do not conform yourselves to the standards of this world, but let God transform you inwardly by a complete change of your mind. Then you will be able to know the will of God—what is good and is pleasing to him and is perfect.

—*Romans 12:2 (TEV)*

God sent his Son, Jesus Christ, into the world so that persons of all ages might be saved and live eternally with him in his Kingdom.

None of us finds it easy to change or be transformed because we are self-centered. Until we are able to overcome our own selfish nature and recognize the need to change, change is not possible for us or those around us.

Our faith and commitment to Jesus Christ can be measured by this question: Is the Jesus of Nazareth I am modeling strong enough to convince others of my faith? Whenever we ask this question, we see the need to be changed continually.

Worship

Adoration: Praising God

Sing the Doxology together.

Praise God from whom all blessings flow;
Praise him all creatures here below;
Praise him above, ye heavenly host;
Praise Father, Son, and Holy Ghost.

Confession: Understanding Us

Father: God, help us to follow you day by day.

Mother: God, help us to see thee more clearly, love thee more dearly, follow thee more nearly.

Children: God, help us to pray daily for your help so that we may have strength and wisdom of faith to do your will in your world.

Affirmation: Growing in Faith

Ask one of the older children to read the following statement:

"Every time we break bread together around the family table, let us remember that God provides daily bread for us to share with others. Let us always remember that as disciples of Christ we are to feed one another with love and affection, just as Christ taught us to do when he walked the hills of Galilee with his friends and disciples. Help us to realize we need to share our lives and help one another to change for the better, just as we share our food to help us sustain one another. Help us to realize that we are never to eat and run off on our own. We are to eat and share our daily bread with others. As we share our lives, we help one another change."

Dedication: Living New Life

Sing or read together the old familiar hymn, "Come into My Heart, Lord Jesus."

Into my heart, into my heart,
Come into my heart, Lord Jesus,
Come in today, come in to stay,
Come into my heart, Lord Jesus.

Rule in my heart, rule in my heart,
Thou King of my heart, Lord Jesus,
Make this thy throne, rule there alone,
Thou King of my heart, Lord Jesus.

Walking with thee, walking with thee,
We're walking with Thee, Lord Jesus,
In work, in play, we serve, we pray,
We're walking with thee, Lord Jesus.

Living Our Worship

Choose one or more of the following:

As a family, think of the ways that you can change—transform—your lives to make your home a better place for all persons who live with your family.

Invite each family member to think of one key trait he or she possesses that is not positive. Ask each to write this trait on a piece of paper. Fold the paper into a little ball and place it in a jar with a lid on it. Use a clear jar and place it on the center of your table. Whenever you gather to eat a meal, each family member will think of the particular trait that she or he wants to change.

Set aside a period of silence before or after your table grace each day. During this silence, invite each member to think about the trait each would most like to change. Invite each person to thank God when he or she has been successful in changing or to ask God for help when he or she has failed to change.

Remembrances

Use the following prayer: "God, thank you for the possibility for life with you and your Son, Jesus of Nazareth. You gave each of us the potential to serve you by faith. Help us to remember we need you every hour of our lives. As life changes around us, we need a constant force to guide us as a compass gives direction. As we travel through life, give us wisdom to move with faith and not fear the unknown. We know you love us. Amen."

WHEN GOOD FRIENDS MOVE

Preparation

We love, because he first loved us.

—1 John 4:19

Just as we are a family whether together or apart, so we remain close to friends who move away. What a good time to celebrate our need for other people and the joys we find in friendship when a family friend moves away! In many ways, we are not saying good-bye but are reaffirming what we have meant to one another and what we will continue to mean to one another.

Worship

Adoration: Praising God

Ask one member to read 1 John 4:7-12. After reading the scripture, all respond with "Thank you, God, for teaching us to love our friends as you love us. Amen."

Confession: Understanding Us

Lead the family in the following prayer: "We thank you, God, for people who are our friends. We especially thank you for *(names),* but we wish them luck and Godspeed to their new home. We believe in your master plan in our lives. You move people in and out of our lives, and we know that each person leaves a unique gift with us. Our lives have been touched by the *(name)* family, and we know we would have been less than complete if we had not enjoyed their friendship. Amen."

Affirmation: Growing in Faith

Plan a family brainstorming session in which each member of the family takes turns sharing memories of the family who is moving. The members will probably want to share some of the "gifts," memories they will always cherish about the family who is moving. Direct the family members to begin by saying, "I remember . . . ," and take turns around the family until they have recalled all the memories they wish to share.

Dedication: Living New Life

As a family, compose a "commission" to the departing family and share it with them. The commission should include your hopes, dreams, good wishes, and plans for the future of the departing family.

Living Our Worship

Choose one or more of the following:

Invite the family that is moving to be your guests for a meal and sharing time in your home. Embrace the departing family and put them in the center of your family's love circle.

Hold a family discussion to decide your family's departure gift to the family. Plan something that will be meaningful to the entire family, perhaps a plant—even one from your home that your family has grown—or a special gift of food, a favorite of the departing family, prepared by your entire family.

Ask each family member to prepare a short note of love and appreciation for one of the members of the departing family. The notes might focus on a specific remembrance or event that occurred with a member of the departing family. Hand deliver these notes to the family.

Remembrances

Help your children recognize the joy, as well as the sadness, of having good friends move away. Plan either to write the family in their new home or to make a long-distance telephone call to the family once they are settled in their new community. They will appreciate your note or phone call during the first weeks of their adjustment to a new community and new friends. Don't let the good times and your valued friendship be lost during the coming years.

LEAVING HOME

Preparation

A time to keep, and a time to cast away.

—Ecclesiastes 3:6

The time when a child (really an adult by now) leaves home to join the service, to take an apartment, to go to college, or to take a new job is painful for the parents and the child. It has been called "tearing away" and in many ways it is tearing. It is starting over again. It is the beginning of a new relationship as adult-adult out of the older parent-child relationship.

Parent and youth share many fears and misgivings. Both are pleased that this stage of life has arrived, but both are a little fearful about the change. It clearly is a time for openness and honesty. It is a time for sharing your feelings. It is a time of rejoicing in the past and a time of hoping for the future.

Worship

Adoration: Praising God

All: To you be the glory and praise, O God.
Parent: God gave you strength.
Youth: May I use my strength to help the weak.
Parent: God gave you courage.
Youth: May I use my courage to help the meek.
Parent: God gave you a brain.
Youth: May I use my intellect wisely.
Parent: God gave you a body.

Youth: May I use my body to help others.
Parent: God gave you wisdom.
All: To you be the glory and praise, O, God.

Confession: Understanding Us

Pray together, "Dear God, we aren't always ready to accept what life offers us. We are all thankful for the time we have had together as a family. Bless our happy times and help us to remember these. But, we are also fearful, O God, about the future. One of us leaves our home as an adult today. Go with *(name)* and bless *(name)*. Help each of us to have the wisdom and courage to support *(name)* and to give *(name)* the freedom *(name)* needs to grow. We ask all of this in the name of your Son who left home and joined us here on earth, Jesus Christ, our Lord. Amen."

Affirmation: Growing in Faith

Read aloud the story of Jesus left in the temple (Luke 2:41-50) and talk about how Mary and Joseph felt and how Jesus felt. What do you suppose Jesus meant by his answer, "I must be in my Father's house"? What is your Father's business to which you must attend?

Dedication: Living New Life

Ask the family members to gather around the youth and, one by one, present a gift. The gift may be a symbol of some good memory or some hope for the future. It might be a special snapshot or picture or favorite food or a love note. Tell the youth to go in peace.

Living Our Worship

Choose one or more of the following:

Plan a farewell party as a send-off for the youth. Make it a festive occasion with lots of noise and gifts. The gifts could be practical items the youth will need. Involve the youth in selecting who is invited, what the menu will be, what will be done for entertainment.

Pack a special survival kit for the youth, containing items that are practical and needed, but often overlooked. For example, consider the contents of a medicine cabinet or a wastebasket of cleaning supplies.

Give the youth a special picture or group portrait of the family.

Select a favorite snapshot and have it enlarged or have all the family members secretly meet for a photo session. Keep the picture a surprise and present it as a going-away gift.

Remembrances

The best way to observe this event is to give your youth enough room to grow and yet enough support to allow that growth. Keep in touch, but don't overdo your attention. Call once in a while or write, but don't expect the youth to return the calls or letters. This is a time of separating. The newly found adult must discover his or her own life-style and make independent decisions.

Remember when you visit your youth in the dormitory or apartment or room, it is not yours. Don't be critical or judgmental. You expect the youth to live according to your standards when in your home; do the same while in his or hers.

Above all else, try to establish an adult relationship with your youth. Discover your youth as an adult friend and enjoy your friendship.

Let your youth know he or she can come home to talk or to get help or just to have someone ready to respond.

ILLNESS

Preparation

"Go," Jesus told him, "your faith has made you well."
—Mark 10:52 (TEV)

We need to be good stewards of God's gifts of life and health. However, there are times when we are ill. Perhaps we must sometime confront an illness from which we cannot be cured. Whether temporary or permanent, illness must be dealt with in faith. Our faith can help us to be made well or to accept our illness with grace.

Worship

Adoration: Praising God

Read or sing together "A Mighty Fortress Is Our God" by Martin Luther:

A mighty fortress is our God,
A bulwark never failing;

Our helper he amid the flood
Of mortal ills prevailing:
For still our ancient foe
Doth seek to work us woe;
His craft and power are great,
And, armed with cruel hate,
On earth is not his equal.

Did we in our own strength confide,
Our striving would be losing,
Were not the right man on our side,
The man of God's own choosing:
Dost ask who that may be?
Christ Jesus, it is he;
Lord Sabaoth, his name,
From age to age the same,
And he must win the battle.

And though this world, with devils filled,
Should threaten to undo us,
We will not fear, for God hath willed
His truth to triumph through us:
The Prince of Darkness grim,
We tremble not for him;
His rage we can endure,
For lo, his doom is sure;
One little word shall fell him.

That word above all earthly powers,
No thanks to them, abideth;
The Spirit and the gifts are ours
Through him who with us sideth:
Let goods and kindred go,
This mortal life also;
The body they may kill:
God's truth abideth still;
His kingdom is forever.

Confession: Understanding Us

Have a member of the family read John 5:1-11. Share as a family your thoughts on verse 6. (Do you want to get well?) Pray together, "Lord, when I don't feel like being healed, help me to remember that the difference between what I am and who you want me to be is what I do! Amen."

Affirmation: Growing in Faith

Have a member of the family read Matthew 25:31-40. Following the reading, have one of the parents remind the family members that whenever we help someone we are doing it for Christ.

Dedication: Living New Life

Have a member of the family read Matthew 14:34-36. Jesus trusts us to touch others with his love and compassion. As we reach out to others in love, we are allowing others around us to know they can still be touched by Jesus' love. Lead the family in prayer: "Lord, help us to lead others to you so that they might be healed by faith through us. Amen."

Living Our Worship

Choose one or more of the following:

Ask your pastor for the name of a person who is suffering from loneliness, so that your family might visit that person and help to heal his or her pain.

Let each family member ask his or her church school teacher for the name of a person who is ill at home. Call the person who is sick or write a note on a get-well card or, if possible, go and visit that person.

As a family, visit a person who has a terminal illness. You will come away being grateful for your own life, and your faith in God will be strengthened.

Remembrances

Remember no matter what the illness may be in your life, your faith can help you face the future with peace. We know not what the future holds, but we know who holds the future! Thanks be to God!

HOSPITALIZATION

Preparation

Peace I leave with you; my peace I give to you; not as the world gives do I give to you. Let not your hearts be troubled, neither let them be afraid.

—John 14:27

Preparing to go to the hospital is a lot like taking a trip. One needs to get ready for the trip physically, mentally, and spiritually. All of us fear places and events that are strange to us, and so it is of vital importance that you do all that is possible to prepare your youngster when a family member or a friend or the youngster is going into the hospital.

In preparing someone for hospitalization, the most important factor is to let the person know that he or she will not be alone. The person needs assurance that friends will visit and that doctors will be persons who merit trust.

Worship

Adoration: Praising God

Parent: Thank you, Lord, for our family.

Child: Thank you, Lord, for loving us as your children. May we always tell one another how much our family means to us.

All: Amen.

Confession: Understanding Us

Invite the children to express whatever impressions they have of hospitals. Listen carefully in order to provide any explanations that are needed.

Affirmation: Growing in Faith

Ask one of the children to read Matthew 6:25. Apply this scripture to your family member who will be admitted into the hospital. Talk about your hopes and fears.

If you do not have a family member or friend entering the hospital, use this time to discuss your attitudes about hospitals, being hospitalized, and visiting those who are in hospitals.

Dedication: Living New Life

Discuss how each person will help around the house while the future patient listens carefully. Everyone doing his or her part around the house will help your patient recover when he or she comes home. Your patient now can expect to concentrate on getting well physically.

Living Our Worship

Choose one or more of the following:

Ask each member to be responsible for giving the patient one gift that will be necessary for the trip to the hospital. A tube of toothpaste, a toothbrush, a new pair of slippers, perhaps a bathrobe might be needed. Also, writing materials are important.

Make a family collage, using family pictures. Be sure to leave room to sign your name and best wishes. For this project, a large piece of poster board would be good.

How about making a card holder out of strips of material or ribbon? The material strip or ribbon can be hung on the wall where the patient can see and enjoy it.

A stuffed animal could be made or purchased for visitors to sign as they come into the patient's room. This would be a constant reminder of the special persons who care for the patient.

Remembrances

Compose a family prayer to thank God for hospitals. Also, thank God for doctors, nurses, family, and friends who care about the patient and are dedicated to the patient's health and welfare.

SUFFERING

Preparation

If one part of the body suffers, all the other parts suffer with it; if one part is praised, all the other parts share its happiness.

—*1 Corinthians 12:26 (TEV)*

In the Christian community of faith, we have the opportunity and responsibility to love and be loved by fellow disciples of Christ. Jesus' life and ministry demonstrated clearly that we need to share our burdens and lighten the load that life sometimes brings our way.

There are many kinds of suffering in this world. Perhaps the most devastating type is loneliness. Often we isolate ourselves from others because we have a problem or do not want to get involved in the problem of another person. We need to remember the message of Jesus: "You are like salt for all mankind" (Matt. 5:13, TEV).

Worship

Adoration: Praising God

Read Psalm 23.

Confession: Understanding Us

Father: God, forgive us when we do not call on you for help and strength.

Mother: God, forgive us when we forget to call on our family members to help us when we are in need.

Children: God, help us to share our problems with one another as well as with you because we know that we cannot deal with our problems alone. Let each member of our family learn to shepherd other family members.

Affirmation: Growing In Faith

Ask a family member to read Luke 9:21-27. Think about this passage and what it says about suffering. Jesus did not promise us that we would not suffer, but he did promise that he would always be with us. Conclude with a prayer thanking God for his help and support for those who suffer.

Dedication: Living New Life

Ask a family member to read Psalm 90:1-6 from the Bible. After reading this prayer on the brevity and sorrow of life, discuss how each individual family member can and should live his or her life to the fullest with the help of God.

Conclude your discussion by singing the Doxology.

Praise God from whom all blessings flow;
Praise him all creatures here below;
Praise him above, ye heavenly host;
Praise Father, Son, and Holy Ghost.

Living Our Worship

Choose one or more of the following:

As a family, think of the ways that you could respond to the suffering of individuals within your household. Think about ways to express a sensitivity that is both supportive and transforming for the person facing a problem.

Identify a person who has lost a loved one or who has a family member in the hospital. Do something for this person to express your love and concern for her or him.

Think about someone you know who may be lonely. Write this person a letter or send a cheerful card.

Remembrances

"Our help is in the name of the Lord, who made heaven and earth" (Psalm 124:8). Lead the family in this prayer: "Lord, when we don't know what else to ask, you hear our prayers for *help.* We know that you will guide us and give us strength to endure and to overcome our earthly trials. Amen."

DEATH

Preparation

I am sure that neither death, nor life . . . will be able to separate us from the love of God in Christ Jesus our Lord.

—Romans 8:38-39

Death is everywhere—plants and animals die; death is on television; it is overheard in conversations. Even the youngest child becomes aware of death as a part of living. Perhaps the ideal time for talking with your children about death is before they have experienced the death of a loved one. A good time to explore death might be around the death of an animal or a pet, although this service is designed to recognize the death of a person.

Whenever the conversations occur, however, it is important that you are honest, simple, and direct. Most of all, the conversations about death need to be shared in an environment of warmth, love, and reassurance. Closeness and involvement convince the child that his or her security is certain; sorrow is more easily faced together.

Worship

Adoration: Praising God

Sing or read together as a family John Fawcett's hymn, "Blest Be the Tie That Binds."

Blest be the tie that binds
Our hearts in Christian love:
The fellowship of kindred minds
Is like to that above.

Before our Father's throne
We pour our ardent prayers;
Our fears, our hopes, our aims are one,
Our comforts and our cares.

We share each other's woes,
Our mutual burdens bear,
And often for each other flows
The sympathizing tear.

When we asunder part,
It gives us inward pain;
But we shall still be joined in heart,
And hope to meet again.

Confession: Understanding Us

As a family, discuss the sadness and grief you feel over this death. Be as honest and open with other members of the family as you can about your sorrow. Think back about your experiences with the deceased and invite each member of the family to reflect on his or her experiences with the deceased. Emphasis might be placed on the happy experiences shared with the deceased so that pleasant images are fresh and constantly being recalled.

Conclude your time with a prayer in which you thank God for the deceased's life and your experiences together. Celebrate how each family member added to the happiness of the deceased's life.

Affirmation: Growing in Faith

As a family, reflect on the meaning of God's plan for our world and for each of us. Consider how each of us has a birth and a death, but we are always in God's love and concern, no matter what happens.

Dedication: Living New Life

Parent: Thanks be to God for *(name of deceased).*

Parent: We thank you, God, for the good times we shared and for the ways we touched each other's lives.

Child: I thank you, God, for the ways I was able to give attention to *(name of deceased).*

(Other children in family repeat above phrase.)

All: Our hurt is lessened, Lord, knowing that *(name of deceased)* is in your love and care and that we all added much to the happiness of *(deceased's name)* life.

Living Our Worship

Choose one or more of the following:

Let each member of the family find an appropriate way to remember the deceased. You might want to collect snapshots or pictures of the deceased and review your shared happiness by looking at the pictures.

Encourage each member of the family to thank God privately for the deceased and to remember him or her in their prayers privately.

Encourage each family member to find a way to comfort other members of the deceased's family. Perhaps a note or card or hand-drawn picture might be appropriate. You might want to pick flowers and take them to other members of the deceased's family.

Encourage members of the family to remember the deceased with a special prayer or a visit to the burial place on the deceased's birthday and at other special occasions.

Remembrances

As a family, read aloud the story of the resurrection of Jesus, Matthew 28:1-20. Talk about all the comfort and joy our faith in Jesus and his resurrection bring to us in times of death. Especially concentrate on the last few words of the scripture: "Lo, I am with you always, to the close of the age." Thank God in prayer for the resurrection of Jesus and for the knowledge that nothing, not even death, can separate us from his love.

V. CELEBRATING SEASONS AND HOLIDAYS

FIRST DAY OF FALL

Preparation

The Lord our God... gives the rain in its season, the autumn rain and the spring rain.

—Jeremiah 5:24

God made our world according to a pattern; the seasons change each year as part of that pattern. Our God is predictable and dependable. These important truths are most easily understood by a young child who views the world of nature and watches the seasons change according to God's plan. Each season brings its own special events and fun times. To recognize the seasons as a gift from God and to be thankful is important to each of us.

Worship

Adoration: Praising God

Child: It is fall. That is good. God gave us the fall.
Parent: The days grow shorter and cooler.
Child: The leaves turn red and gold and orange and yellow.
Parent: The leaves fall on the ground.
Child: You can rake and pile the leaves and hide and jump in them.
Parent: It is a time for the animals to store up food—
Child: For the squirrels to collect nuts and prepare for winter.
Parent: It is a time for the birds to prepare to fly south.
All: It is fall. That is good. God gave us the fall.

Confession: Understanding Us

Invite each member to talk about why he or she does not like the fall. Let each person celebrate summer and remember the joys and the fun of the warm weather. After all the family has talked about what they dislike about fall, end the conversation with, "For everything there is a season. God gave us our seasons and they are good. Amen."

Affirmation: Growing in Faith

Invite each member to think of fun and joyful things about fall. See how long a list you can make. You might include cooler nights, seeing friends who have been away, watching animals prepare for winter, beautiful colors and leaves to jump in. End the conversation with, "For everything there is a season. God gave us our seasons and they are good. Amen."

Dedication: Living New Life

Ask an older child or a parent to read Ecclesiastes 3:1-8.

Living Our Worship

Choose one or more of the following:

Ask each family member to plan and help prepare for a "Welcome Fall" party. Invite another family or two to attend or involve only your own family. Plan the food around special fall treats, such as apples and nuts and popcorn. Use the fall colors and leaves to decorate the table and plan indoor fall activities for the family.

Plan a "Farewell Summer, Welcome Fall" picnic. Choose a beautiful fall day and take a picnic meal to an outdoor setting. As you enjoy the food, talk about the changes in nature and observe what is happening around you. A walk in the woods or a hike in nearby areas would be a good conclusion.

Remembrances

Involve the family as a group in planning how to celebrate the fall. Do they want to rake leaves together or prepare the garden for winter? Consider helping an elderly or ill neighbor prepare for fall by washing and installing storm windows or preparing the yard for winter.

BEGINNING OF FALL SCHEDULES

Preparation

Come to me, all of you who are tired from carrying heavy loads, and I will give you rest. Take my yoke and put it on you, and learn from me, because I am gentle and humble in spirit; and you will find rest. For the yoke I will give you is easy, and the load I will put on you is light. —*Matthew 11:28-30* (TEV)

In thinking of fall, plan to learn more about God to enhance the faith of family members. What better way is there to approach our busy hours, days, months, and seasons than by learning together about the God who loves and cares for us?

Worship

Adoration: Praising God

Ask Mom or Dad to read Proverbs 7:1-4. Then discuss how you can work together to keep the teachings of Jesus Christ as the center of your thoughts during the fall and winter months of this year.

Confession: Understanding Us

As a family, sing or read together the familiar American folk hymn, "Lord, I Want to Be a Christian."

Lord, I want to be a Christian
in my heart, in my heart;
Lord, I want to be a Christian
in my heart, in my heart,
In my heart, in my heart,
Lord, I want to be a Christian
in my heart.

Lord, I want to be more loving
in my heart, in my heart;
Lord, I want to be more loving
in my heart, in my heart.
In my heart, in my heart,
Lord, I want to be more loving
in my heart.

Lord, I want to be more holy
in my heart; in my heart;
Lord, I want to be more holy
in my heart, in my heart.
In my heart, in my heart,
Lord, I want to be more holy
in my heart.

Lord, I want to be like Jesus
in my heart, in my heart;
Lord, I want to be like Jesus
in my heart, in my heart.

In my heart, in my heart,
Lord, I want to be like Jesus
in my heart.

Following this hymn, talk about how you can be more Christian.

Affirmation: Growing in Faith

Take a large calendar or date book and fill in your family's activities and commitments. Encourage the children to include their dates and special events on the calendar.

Dedication: Living New Life

After you have filled in the important dates and times, dedicate your family schedule to God with this statement:

> 'God, You are the Giver of our talents and our responsibilities. As we dedicate our fall schedule, help us to keep our thoughts centered on you as the source of our strength and insiration.

By building the prayer together, each person is affirming God as their Lord and covenanting to share the burdens and joys of life together as a family. This prayer can help your family grow together in your understanding of how to share life in the household of faith.

Living Our Worship

Choose one or more of the following:

Plan to make something special for another member of the family. Draw names out of a cup or bowl. Then invite each member to make a symbol of fall for the person whose name was drawn.

On the weekend after the first day of fall, enjoy a leisurely breakfast as you recall summertime fun and anticipate fall family events.

Take a picture of your family at your favorite spot in the house and mount it on a bulletin board in the kitchen or on the refrigerator door. Surround the photo with symbols of fall that remind you of activities your family enjoys doing. Don't forget to include such tasks as school, housework, and so forth.

Make a list of questions about nature your family would like to explore during the fall season, such as the process by which leaves turn from green to brilliant reds, yellows, browns.

Remembrances

Allow time for each member to share the joys and the troubles of settling into his or her routine. We all need support and encouragement in accepting the routine, and we all need listening ears.

End your discussion with the song, "Take the Name of Jesus with You," by Lydia Baxter.

Take the name of Jesus with you,
Child of sorrow and of woe;
It will joy and comfort give you;
Take it, then, where'er you go.

Take the name of Jesus ever,
As a shield from every snare;
If temptations round you gather,
Breathe that holy name in prayer.

O the precious name of Jesus!
How it thrills our souls with joy,
When his loving arms receive us,
And his songs our tongues employ!

At the name of Jesus bowing,
Falling prostrate at his feet,
King of kings in heaven we'll crown him,
When our journey is complete.

Chorus:
Precious name, O how sweet!
Hope of earth and joy of heaven;
Precious name, O how sweet!
Hope of earth and joy of heaven.

HALLOWEEN

Preparation

Make a joyful noise to the Lord.

—*Psalm 98:4*

It is important for us as Christians to provide opportunities to express ourselves creatively and to relax. Spontaneity and joy are two of the finest traits of a truly Christian person. Too often we approach life seriously and somberly in our desire to be mature Christians.

Halloween comes to us from the ancient Druid custom of celebrating the end of their year on October 31. The Druids believed that everything in nature was filled with a spirit: animals, rocks, trees. Some of the spirits were good, some evil. Centuries later, the Christian religion gave us our name *Halloween* from Allhallowmas (November 1), the festival dedicated to the saints.

Halloweens of early years were filled with fear because people really believed in what we now know are folklore and superstition. Even though we have kept many of the old customs alive this one night of the year, we have made the evening a time of fun and merrymaking.

Worship

Adoration: Praising God

Read in parts Issac Watts's hymn, "Jesus Shall Reign."

Mother: Jesus shall reign where'er the sun
Does his successive journeys run;
His kingdom spread from shore to shore,
Till moons shall wax and wane no more.

Father: To him shall endless prayer be made,
And endless praises crown his head;
His name like sweet perfume shall rise
With every morning sacrifice.

First Child: People and realms of every tongue
Dwell on his love with sweetest song,
And infant voices shall proclaim
Their early blessings on his name.

Second Child: Blessings abound where'er he reigns;
The prisoner leaps to loose his chains;
The weary find eternal rest,
And all the sons of want are blest.

All: Let every creature rise and bring

His grateful honors to our King;
Angels descend with sons again,
And earth repeat the loud amen!
(Based on Psalm 72)

Confession: Understanding Us

During this part of worship, one parent can begin the following prayer and invite the other members to add to it: "Dear God, you have made us and we are yours. You want us to be happy and to worship you with great joy at all times and in all places. But sometimes our fears stop us, O Lord, from being happy and joyful. We are afraid of. . . ." (Family members add their particular fears.) "Help us to overcome our fears and to know that you are with us always. Amen."

Affirmation: Growing in Faith

Ask each member to write out a fear on a piece of paper. The older members may need to help the younger members of the family write. Instruct each member to crumble the paper and throw it away saying, "God gives us the power to overcome our fears. Fears be gone! In Jesus' name, Amen."

Dedication: Living New Life

Parent: It's Halloween. It's an evening for dressing up as ghosts, witches, and other fearsome creatures. It's an evening for a parade to nearby streets.

Older Child: It's Halloween. It's an evening for going door to door for gifts of fruit, candy or cookies.

Parent: It's an evening for giving up fears and being joyful in the Lord.

Older Child: "These things I have spoken to you, that my joy may be in you, and that your joy may be full" (John 15:11). Amen.

Living Our Worship

Choose one or more of the following:

Plan a Halloween party for your family. Invite several other families to help you celebrate. Carry out the traditions of wearing costumes; eating popcorn, cider and doughnuts; and ducking for apples. Enjoy yourselves in fantasy.

Plan for one parent to dress as a Halloween character and sit on the front porch quietly. As neighborhood children come to the door for trick or treat, talk in a deep voice or make eerie noises. The whole family can enjoy the preparations and watching the surprised children's reactions.

Plan a meal of all of the children's favorite foods either before or after the trick or treating time. Allow each child to invite one friend.

Remembrances

As you unwind from the evening of excitement and prepare the children for bed, discuss how much fun it is to pretend that you are a ghost or witch or monster. Help each to realize that by laughing at our fears and by acknowledging that we have them—it's all right to be afraid; we all are afraid of something—we make our fears less frightening. Be sure each child understands that no matter how frightened we are, God is with us and loves and protects us.

THANKSGIVING

Preparation

O give thanks to the Lord, for he is good, for his steadfast love endures for ever.

—Psalm 136:1

Celebrations of Thanksgiving occurred much earlier in history than in the generation of our forefathers the Pilgrims. Thanksgiving ceremonies are described in the Old Testament (Exodus 23:16; Leviticus 23:34). During the Feast of Tabernacles the Hebrews reminded themselves of their wanderings in the desert. The American Indians observed annual days of giving thanks long before Europeans arrived on this continent.

Today our Thanksgiving celebration not only helps us remember the bounty we have, but it also shows our appreciation for our forefathers and our religious heritage. Most of all, at Thanksgiving we give thanks for God, our supreme gift.

Worship

Adoration: Praising God

Invite a family member to read aloud Psalm 90. Ask another to read aloud the first three verses of Isaac Watts's interpretation of Psalm 90, "O God, Our Help in Ages Past."

O God, our help in ages past,
Our hope for years to come,
Our shelter from the stormy blast,
And our eternal home!

Under the shadow of the throne
Still may we dwell secure;
Sufficient is thine arm alone,
And our defense is sure.

Before the hills in order stood,
Or earth received her frame,
From everlasting thou art God,
To endless years the same.

Confession: Understanding Us

Father: O Lord, we pray for our family and our home.
First Child: We pray for those who are sometimes sad.
Second Child: We pray for moments of joy.
Mother: We pray for those who feel misunderstood.
First Child: We thank you for our talents and strengths.
Second Child: We pray for our weaknesses.
Father: We thank you, God, for making each of us special.
All: For all your gifts, we thank you, O Lord.

Affirmation: Growing in Faith

Share as a family aspects of life for which each is thankful. Include your health, nature, country, colors, food, imaginations, and feelings. Encourage each person to offer a prayer of thanks for one gift he or she has mentioned.

Dedication: Living New Life

Encourage each person to go to one other member and say, "Thank you for being you." After each person has said thanks, let the entire family join in the sentence, "Thank you, God, for giving us each member of our family. Amen."

Living Our Worship

Choose one or more of the following:

Allow the children to prepare for Thanksgiving by including them in the family plans. Perhaps small children would want to decorate special napkin rings (cardboard centers of toilet tissue rolls can be cut to size and decorated). Elementary school children can help plan the menu and prepare the food. The children might decorate the house, make the centerpiece for the table, or design place cards.

Help elementary school children look up early celebrations of Thanksgiving and prepare a statement about how others have given thanks to God. The library will provide information about the Jewish Festival of Tabernacles and American Indian customs. Read Judges 9:27 to see how the children of Israel gave thanks.

Invite a person who is alone for the holidays to join your family for Thanksgiving dinner. You may want to invite an elderly person without family or with a distant family to be "grandparent for a day." Make the day truly festive and joyous.

Find a worthy cause in your community to which your family might contribute funds. As Thanksgiving approaches, agree upon how the family will collect money. Each member may wish to donate, or the entire family may vote to give up a meal or a luxury and donate the money. We cannot just *say* thanks but must also *do* thanks "with heart and hands and voices."

Remembrances

Ask each member to write something for which he or she wishes to thank another person on a slip of paper and put the paper away as a reminder to thank that person. The older members can help the younger children write these reminders. Encourage each member to thank the person mentioned in his or her note.

FIRST SUNDAY IN ADVENT

Preparation

And this will be a sign for you: you will find a babe wrapped in swaddling cloths and lying in a manger.

—Luke 2:12

Advent means "arrival" or "coming" and marks the coming of Jesus into the world. The Advent season begins four Sundays before Christmas. It is appropriate that this preparation time revolves around the home.

The words of the great Christmas carol by Isaac Watts—music by Handel—"Joy to the World" state most clearly what our task is as we prepare for the birthday of Christ and its meaning for our lives:

Joy to the world! the Lord is come:
Let earth receive her King;
Let every heart prepare him room,
And heaven and nature sing,
And heaven and nature sing,
And heaven, and heaven and nature sing.

Remember, wherever we receive him, the Christ enters in. May God grant you and your family a most blessed Christmas as you prepare for his reentry into your home.

Worship

Adoration: Praising God

Sing or read the great Christmas carol, "Joy to the World."

Joy to the world! the Lord is come:
Let earth receive her King;
Let every heart prepare him room,
And heaven and nature sing,
And heaven and nature sing,
And heaven, and heaven and nature sing.

Joy to the world! the Saviour reigns:
Let men their songs employ;

While fields and floods, rocks, hills, and plains
Repeat the sounding joy,
Repeat the sounding joy,
Repeat, repeat the sounding joy.

No more let sins and sorrows grow,
Nor thorns infest the ground;
He comes to make his blessings flow
Far as the curse is found,
Far as the curse is found,
Far as, far as the curse is found.

He rules the world with truth and grace,
And makes the nations prove
The glories of his righteousness,
And wonders of his love,
And wonders of his love,
And wonders, wonders of his love.

Confession: Understanding Us

Father: O God, hear our prayer of confession.

Mother: Help us to prepare room for your Son and our Lord in our hearts during this Advent season.

Child: May we never forget that it is better to give than to receive gifts.

Father: Often we are so busy with the frills of the Christmas season that we forget the true meaning of the advent of your Son.

All: Lord, we want to prepare for your son's birth in our lives so that we might see him more clearly, follow him more nearly, and love him more dearly each day.

Affirmation: Growing in Faith

Ask a family member to read Isaiah 9:6-7 and 11:1-9. Both of these prophecies have been related to Jesus. As a family, talk about what your dreams and hopes would be for the world. Discuss how the birth of Jesus has changed the world and what future events still need to be accomplished to fulfill these ancient prophecies.

Dedication: Living New Life

Sing or read the Christmas carol, "O Young and Fearless Prophet," by S. Ralph Harlow.

O young and fearless Prophet
of ancient Galilee:
Thy life is still a summons
to serve humanity,
To make our thoughts and actions
less prone to please the crowd,
To stand with humble courage
for truth with hearts uncowed.

O help us walk unflinching
in paths that lead to peace,
Where justice conquers violence
and wars at last shall cease;
O grant that love of country
may help us hear his call,
Who would unite the nations
in brotherhood for all.

O young and fearless Prophet,
we need thy presence here,
Amid our pride and glory
to see thy face appear;
Once more to hear thy challenge
above our noisy day,
Again to lead us forward
along God's holy way.

Living Our Worship

Choose one or more of the following:

Consider making an Advent calendar for your home. By using this method of telling the story of Jesus' birth, the children can help to unfold the actual events that led up to that first Christmas Day.

Consider making an Advent and Christmas banner out of felt or old scraps of material available around the house. Hang your banner in a central place where all can see and enjoy it.

Consider making an Advent wreath for your dinner table out of boughs of greenery. To get the most out of your Advent wreath use the Advent calendar of scripture lessons your church passes out or obtain one at a Christian book supply store.

Help the family see how their own efforts can prepare their hearts for the coming Jesus. Make a crib out of a shoe box and decorate the outside of the box with Christmas cards. Invite each family member to place one piece of straw or yellow yarn in the crib for every kind act he or she does during the day. Place the figure of the Child in the crib on Christmas Eve. By that time the crib should be filled with bedding.

Remembrances

Gather in a circle with your family holding hands. Encourage each member to share the special meanings of Advent during a prayer. May each member of the family wait, believe, hope and grow in faith during this Advent season.

FIRST DAY OF WINTER

Preparation

Thou hast made summer and winter.

—Psalm 74:17

As we grow older, we tend to ignore the praise and recognition of God as creator of our world and of each of us. The change of seasons and a recognition of the pattern and rhythm of God's creation is a perfect time to pause and praise God for creation. Most children love the winter and its activities of snowballs and sledding and skating and Christmas. Their recognition that this is God's good gift to us is helpful and natural for children.

Worship

Adoration: Praising God

Each family member can finish a litany of praise to God by completing the sentence, "O God, I thank you for winter because ________ ________________________________." Some members of the family may have more than one ending. Jot down all the completed sentences and then ask each member to read his or her sentence in turn.

Confession: Understanding Us

Pray together: "O Lord, who created all the world and its seasons, thank you for the season of winter, for boots and heavy coats, mittens and snowmen. Thank you for the snow and ice and cold and a time for nature to rest before the spring. Thank you for icicles and snowflakes and sleds and skates. For the opportunity to share in winter and your plan for the world, we thank you, O Lord. Amen."

Affirmation: Growing in Faith

Ask one member to read Psalm 104:1, 10-23. Invite the family to talk about what winter means to all the creations of God, especially to those mentioned in this portion of the psalm. What happens to the springs of water? the birds? the grasses? the cattle? the plants? the trees? the sun and moon? Help each member identify the changes in God's world.

Dedication: Living New Life

Read together this passage from Genesis 8:22: "While the earth remains, seedtime and harvest, cold and heat, summer and winter, day and night, shall not cease." Amen.

Living Our Worship

Choose one or more of the following:

Design a special symbol for winter, such as a snowflake or snowball. Mount this symbol on the refrigerator door so that the entire family can remember that the season has changed.

Plan a family day of fun and fellowship around one of your favorite winter activities, such as sledding or skiing or ice skating.

Plan an evening around the fireplace for the family. Invite the family to pop corn in the fireplace or to roast hot dogs and marshmallows and share all their feelings about winter. Discuss your plans for celebrating Christmas and who will help with each preparation.

Remembrances

As the children go to bed for the night, suggest that together you thank God for the season of winter and God's many good gifts.

CHRISTMAS

Preparation

To us a child is born, to us a son is given. —*Isaiah 9:6*

Just as the people of long ago waited and prepared and rejoiced in the fulfillment of God's promise, so we too have waited and prepared to celebrate joyfully the birth of Christ.

God has come to us in the Messiah. He came in the quiet of the night and was first visited by poor shepherds who offered him their love and devotion. We celebrate because Christ is born. We celebrate because God's love is manifested in this birth.

Worship

Praise Affirming God

Read or sing together "Love Came Down at Christmas" by Christina G. Rossetti.

Love came down at Christmas,
Love all lovely, Love divine;
Love was born at Christmas;
Star and angels gave the sign.

Worship we the Godhead,
Love incarnate, Love divine;
Worship we our Jesus,
But wherewith for sacred sign?

Love shall be our token;
Love be yours and love be mine,
Love to God and all men,
Love for plea and gift and sign.

Confession: Understanding Us

All: Let us pray.

Parent: Let us pray that we may all have a merry and blessed Christmas.

All: Hear our prayer, baby Jesus.

Child: Let us pray that we may find the real meaning of Christmas in giving to others.

All: Hear our prayer, baby Jesus.

Parent: Let us pray that the hungry may be fed and the lonely find comfort this Christmas.

All: Hear our prayer, baby Jesus.

Child: Let us pray that the peace of Christ may be in our hearts, in our families, and in the world.

All: Hear our prayer, baby Jesus. Amen.

Adoration: Growing in Faith

Ask a member to read Isaiah 9:5-7 and 11:6-7. Talk about this prophecy of the Messiah and how Jesus fulfilled this dream. Encourage even the youngest child to struggle with this vision of a new world where the wolf and lamb, the calf and lion shall be at peace and led by a little child. Talk as a family about what these images mean for today and how your family might find greater peace and tranquility. Conclude with a prayer to thank God for the gift of the peacemaker, Jesus.

Dedication: Living New Faith

Join in the following unison prayer: "God, our Father, thank you for the birth of your Son. You kept your promise to persons long ago and sent him as our leader. Help us today to follow his teachings of love and giving. Amen."

Living Our Worship

Choose one or more of the following:

Take a small Christmas tree and decorate it with little notes. Ask each family member to make a wish for every other member of the family or for the world. Write each wish on a slip of paper and attach it to the tree on Christmas Eve. Later undress the tree by having each member of the family select a slip of paper and read it to the rest of the family.

Make chrismons cut out of paper or cardboard to symbolize Jesus and his ministry and hang them on your tree. You might make a cross or a shepherd's crook or a star to symbolize Jesus.

Read the Christmas story from Luke 2:1-6 as your family puts out its manger scene. Talk about how the persons in Bethlehem must have felt when Jesus was born.

As a family, select a needy person or a charity that your family might help. You need not give money, but might donate homemade food or give of your family's special skills or talents or just share your time.

Remembrances

Read Romans 12:1 and talk about what Paul might have had in mind when he wrote this passage. Talk about how your family can truly worship God and the Christ this Christmas season.

WEEK AFTER CHRISTMAS

Preparation

The righteous flourish like the palm tree, and grow like a cedar in Lebanon. —*Psalm 92:12*

The week after Christmas is a letdown. Little is said or done to help a family through the Christmas aftermath. The holiday spirit still grips the children, but the parents may be tired of the celebration. However, this week can be of real significance for your entire family as you pause *after* the event of Christmas and recelebrate that happiest and most complete of all days, the birth of Jesus Christ.

Worship

Adoration: Praising God

For this litany, the parents ask the questions, and the children respond.

Parent: How was your Christmas?
Child:
Parent: Is the tree always in one special place?
Child:
Parent: Do you like to keep the Christmas tree up after Christmas day?
Child:
Parent: What did you like best about our Christmas tree this year?
Child:

Confession: Understanding Us

Pray together: "God, Christmas means different things to different people. To some it means little; to others it means only receiving. Help us to realize the real meaning of Christmas. The real meaning is found in giving and in living. Christ came to bring love and peace to each of us. Help us to celebrate his birth by giving those same gifts of love and peace to others. Amen."

Affirmation: Growing in Faith

Read the story of the Magi in Matthew 2:1-12. Discuss with the family how individuals brought gifts to Jesus: the shepherds, the Magi, the animals. Stress that even our symbol of Christmas, the Christmas tree, gives us presents. Talk about what these gifts are—furniture, houses, paper, pears, peaches, maple sugar, canoes, chewing gum, fires in the fireplace, chocolate. God has given us many wonderful and important gifts in the creation of trees.

Dedication: Living New Life

Pray together: "Our Father, what can we possibly give your Son? We aren't rich like the Magi and don't have products to give like the Christmas tree. But, we can give our part. We can give our heart. Amen."

Living Our Worship

Choose one or more of the following:

Visit an art museum or science museum with the family. Many times such museums have special Christmas shows that add interest and value to the family celebration of Christmas.

Invite family members to discover how they can give themselves away to someone else this week. Each person might give time or talents or interests or love to someone outside the family who really needs another person who cares.

Create family name chains to hang on your tree. Make the paper chain of strips of colored paper looped together and then write one member's name on each loop. Include all the aunts and uncles and cousins and everyone you love and remember as part of a family Christmas celebration.

Remembrances

Help each member of the family remember what they really liked about this year's Christmas celebration—a gift or a party or a card or a special phone call. Help each member find a way to say thank you for the gift. We all need to be reminded of that most important gift, Jesus Christ. Thank God for the gift of his Son.

NEW EXPERIENCES

Preparation

Then Jesus said to them, "Do not be afraid."

—Matthew 28:10

As part of your celebration of the New Year, take a look at the new experiences that some or all of your family members may have. Talking about new experiences frees us to share our hopes and fears. Through honest sharing with our loved ones, we confront the fears of the unknown and are able to gather confidence to try the new.

Young children need to know that we adults are sometimes fearful of new experiences. By showing ourselves to be fearful and cautious at times, we enable our children to better understand the normal feelings involved in trying new experiences.

Worship

Adoration: Praising God

Talk about the new year and all the new experiences that await the family. Conclude by thanking God for all the coming new experiences.

Confession: Understanding Us

Ask an adult member to describe how he or she feared doing something. Promise to support and love each family member as he or she tries a new experience.

Affirmation: Growing in Faith

Invite each member to talk about what faith means. You might use such symbols as a building foundation or an umbrella to explain what faith means. As a family, try to develop a definition of faith that helps you try new experiences.

Dedication: Living New Life

Read Hebrews 11:1 and compare this definition of faith to your family's definition. Conclude with a prayer thanking God for the gift of faith as we try new experiences.

Living Our Worship

Choose one or more of the following:

As a family, pretend that you are the relatives of Abraham when God tells Abraham to move to a strange land (Genesis 12:1-3). Talk about your fears and apprehensions. Talk about how God helped Abraham and his family to face this new experience.

Give each member a balloon. Blow up the balloons and help each member write one of his or her fears or apprehensions about a new experience on a balloon. Thank God for the strength to overcome fears and apprehensions. Following the prayer, break the balloons as a symbol of God's removing your fears and doubts.

Remembrances

Ask a good reader to read Psalm 121 for the rest of your family. Conclude with silent prayer, thanking God for being our help and security.

COLD AND WINTER REST

Preparation

While the earth remains, seedtime and harvest, cold and heat, summer and winter, day and night, shall not cease.

—*Genesis 8:22*

Winter is a time to be mindful of the wonder of God's creation through nature. In summer it is easy to believe that the trees, plants, and grass are alive because we can see the green foliage and their blossoms, but it is harder for us to grasp that they are alive in winter when the foliage is gone and all is dormant. Winter is a time to rest and renew ourselves as families. Take advantage of this special time of year to draw closer to one another. Don't be fooled by winter; it is a time to grow.

Worship

Praise: Affirming God

Read or sing together the famous hymn, "In the Bleak Midwinter," by Christina G. Rossetti.

In the bleak midwinter,
Frosty wind made moan,
Earth stood hard as iron,
Water like a stone;
Snow had fallen, snow on snow,
Snow on snow,
In the bleak midwinter,
Long ago.

What can I give him,
Poor as I am?
If I were a shepherd,
I would bring a lamb;
If I were a wise man,
I would do my part;
Yet what can I give him:
Give my heart.

Confession: Understanding Us

Father: Let us pray.

All: Lord, hear our prayer.

Mother: Let us pray that we may use this new year as a time to look at the possibilities and challenges for our family rather than dwelling on old problems.

All: Lord, hear our prayer.

Child: Let us pray that we may love instead of being hateful, forgive instead of holding grudges, be loyal instead of rebellious, be kind instead of selfishly cruel.

All: Lord, hear our prayer.

Father: Let us pray that we may start afresh to live for thee because we love each other as you love us.

All: Lord, hear our prayer.

Adoration: Growing in Faith

Ask a member to read Second Corinthians 5:17. Then discuss how the new year is like the church rituals of baptism or dedication. We are given a new way to live, a new life. We are changed and can never be the same again, if we believe that in loving others we show love for Christ.

Dedication: Living New Life

Pray together: "Dear God, 'No longer do we serve in the old way of a written law, but in the new way of the Spirit.' Amen." (Romans 7:6, TEV).

Living Our Worship

Choose one or more of the following:

Make a family "help list." Pretend you are going shopping together for the best year yet as a family. Ask each member to think of one act he or she could consider doing for you that would help make life more enjoyable. Talk about these suggestions to invite commitment.

Ask each member to think of a job around the house that he or she could do for each family member until the first day of spring. Try to think of something simple and yet meaningful.

Remembrances

Sing the hymn, "A Charge to Keep I Have," by Charles Wesley.

A charge to keep I have,
A God to glorify,
A never dying soul to save,
And fit it for the sky.

To serve the present age,
My calling to fulfill;
O may it all my powers engage
To do my Master's will!

VALENTINE'S DAY

Preparation

God is love, and he who abides in love abides in God, and God abides in him.

—*1 John 4:16*

Someone once said, "All the world loves a lover." Valentine's

Day is the celebration for lovers. It is important for each of us to remember why we love and who first taught us to love. God loved us before we learned to love anyone else and it is this love that we reflect in our human relationships and in our relationship with God.

God gave us the model for love and taught us how to love through his actions toward us. All of our human efforts at love are mere reflections of God's love.

Worship

Adoration: Praising God

Males: Love comes from God.
Females: We love one another.
Males: Because God first loved us.
Females: God showed us how to love one another.
Males: By first loving us.
Females: God loves us.
Males: Therefore, we love one another.
Females: Love comes from God.
All: God is love.

Confession: Understanding Us

Pray together: "God, you are our model for love. You taught us how to love, and you showed us what it meant to love. When we fail to love as you have shown us, we are sorry and ask your forgiveness. Renew our love for one another, God, by showing us again how to love. Teach us to love more perfectly and more completely. We ask this in the name of your Son, who showed us your love on earth. Amen."

Affirmation: Growing in Faith

Ask one member to read John 13:34. Discuss what this Bible verse means. Start the discussion by letting the youngest member of the family speak first and so on until the oldest has spoken last.

Dedication: Living New Life

Conclude your moments of worship by asking each member of the family to go to the other members in turn and, holding hands, look each in the face and say, "I love you, *(name),* because ____________ ______________________________."

After all the family members have shared with one another, join hands and shout, "I love you," in unison.

Living Our Worship

Choose one or more of the following:

Cut out a big red paper valentine. Invite each family member to paste her or his snapshot on the heart and write the words, "Love Lives Here." Hang the valentine on your front door to greet all your visitors and to remind yourselves of your love for one another.

Pass a candy dish filled with the candy hearts with sayings on them around the family and ask each person to select one heart from the dish. Taking turns around the table, ask each member to describe an incident in which the saying on the candy was demonstrated in your family.

Ask each member to write a special valentine greeting to another family member. The valentine should express a time when the family member felt truly loved by the person receiving the greeting. Place these valentines under each person's dinner plate and have everyone read his or her valentine before the meal. Conclude with grace for the meal.

Have everyone write a "love" letter to another member of the family. Hide the letter where you are sure only the recipient will find it (such as on top of the socks in his or her dresser drawer). Invite the members at dinnertime to describe how they felt when they found their letters.

Remembrances

Valentine's Day can lose any meaning for our faith if we get caught up in how many valentines we send or how many people remember us on Valentine's Day. Help your children understand that the reason we love is that God is love and has taught us how to love one another.

Gather around the supper table or in the family room and share your valentine greetings with all your family. Let everyone see and read your cards. Try to remember other people who might be lonely or neglected on this day. If there is still time, decide as a family who might really appreciate a Valentine's Day greeting from you.

Help the children understand how they can *share* all the love they felt on this Valentine's Day with other people tomorrow and the day after and the day after. "All the world loves a lover." Let's all be lovers.

ASH WEDNESDAY

Preparation

Whoever wants to save his own life will lose it; but whoever loses his life for me and for the gospel will save it.

—*Mark 8:35* (*TEV*)

Ash Wednesday is the first day of Lent, which is determined by counting back forty days from Easter Sunday, not including Sundays. Easter is always the first Sunday after the first full moon following the vernal equinox (the first day of spring). Traditionally on this day, ashes have been placed on the foreheads of Christians as a symbol of the beginning of the penitential season. Although ashes are not placed on the foreheads of Christians today in many Protestant churches, the practice is still looked upon as a ritual with deep religious significance.

Worship

Adoration: Praising God

Read or sing together the famous hymn, "O Master, Let Me Walk with Thee," by Washington Gladden.

O Master, let me walk with thee
In lowly paths of service free;
Tell me thy secret; help me bear
The strain of toil, the fret of care.

Help me the slow of heart to move
By some clear, winning world of love;
Teach me the wayward feet to stay,
And guide them in the homeward way.

Teach me thy patience; still with thee
In closer, dearer company,
In work that keeps faith sweet and strong,
In trust that triumphs over wrong;

In hope that sends a shining ray
Far down the future's broadening way;

In peace that only thou canst give,
With thee, O Master, let me live.

Confession: Understanding Us

Use this prayer: "Lord, this generation is the generation we call ours. Help us to live in the generation that we call yours. Help us to understand that instead of acting in selfish ways, we need to have your hand of love, your voice of love, your heart of love, and your mind of love in all we do and say. Amen."

Affirmation: Growing in Faith

Ask a member to read Mark 4:1-9. Talk as a family about what this passage says to us about listening to the word of God, understanding the word of God, and sharing the word of God with others.

Dedication: Living New Life

Read this prayer in unison: "Lord, help us dedicate ourselves during this Lenten season of preparation for new life with your son, Jesus Christ. Help us to be aware that we need to be the hands, voice, heart, and mind of love in this world of insensitivity toward others. Make us more like your Son, Lord, so that others may know you. Amen."

Living Our Worship

Choose one or more of the following:

"The hands of love" (first week). Write a letter each day of the week to a friend. Tell someone how much you appreciate him or her.

"The voice of love" (second week). Telephone someone each day of the week for a short chat just to say what he or she means to you.

"The deed of love" (third week). Take something you have made to two or three friends who mean a great deal to your family.

"The heart of love" (fourth week). Make a prayer list of persons for whom you will pray daily this week. Make sure you include your enemies as well as your friends.

"The mind of love" (fifth week). Pray for yourself each day this week. Read one of the Gospels and learn more about the life of Jesus and how his life and teachings speak to your life.

"The victory of love" (sixth week). This is a week to celebrate.

Invite friends for a potluck meal. You symbolize the body of Christ—in which each of us is a part that gives life to all other parts—when you bring food to the shared meal.

Remembrances

Thank God for all the love he has shown us through his Son.

FIRST DAY OF SPRING

Preparation

His favor is like the clouds that bring the spring rain.

—Proverbs 16:15

The changing of the seasons gives each of us an opportunity to reflect on what it means to be a part of God's creation. We see God's creative power at work as winter leaves and spring arrives. Spring is a season of family fun, joy, good spirits, and exciting plans. We pause to thank God for another season of the year, grateful for the opportunities that spring and nicer weather bring to us as families.

The rhythm and predictability of God's creation are especially appreciated as the seasons change. The warmth of the sun, the flowers, birds, and newfound life are all opportunities for us to thank God for his blessings to us.

Worship

Adoration: Praising God

Parent: You gave us winter, O God.
Child: You give us spring, O God.
Parent: You gave us cold and snow, our Creator.
Child: You give us warmth and sun, our Creator.
Parent: You gave us short days and long nights.
Child: You give us long days and short nights.
Parent: You gave the birds and plants a rest, O God.
Child: You give the birds a new song and plants new flowers, O God.
Parent: You gave us the winter which has passed.
Child: You give us the spring which is just beginning.
All: For both winter and spring we thank you, our Creator.

Confession: Understanding Us

Ask a member to read Hosea 6:3. Pray together: "Dear God, we don't always appreciate all your good gifts. You have given us so much that sometimes we forget where these good gifts originate. Help us to welcome the spring. We welcome the warmth and the sun. We welcome the birds and animals and plants and flowers. We welcome the reawakening of the earth. May this spring be a time of true celebration. May it be a time of laughing, playing, running, and sharing with one another and with you, O God. Amen."

Adoration: Growing in Faith

As a family, talk about what you like about spring. Close the discussion with an informal prayer thanking God for all the aspects you have mentioned.

Dedication: Living New Life

Spring is the season of new life, when flowers bloom and the grass comes alive again. It is the season when new babies are born to animals and when the world awakes from winter's sleep. Ask each member to conclude the worship moments with a silent prayer about why he or she is happy spring has arrived. After a few minutes of silence, pronounce, "Amen."

Living Our Worship

Choose one or more of the following:

Create a banner or streamer to place in your front window or on your front porch or door saying "Welcome, Spring."

Make spring flowers out of paper. Invite each child to paste his or her picture—snapshot or drawing—in the center of a flower. All the flowers can be gathered into a flower pot (either an actual flower pot or a paper one). Label the flower pot with your family's name and talk with each child about how he or she "blooms" within the family.

Make a maypole by running streamers of colored paper from a center pole or tree. Ask the family members to mark each streamer with the name of something for which they are thankful. Weave the streamers together as a visual prayer of thanks for the arrival of spring.

Remembrances

As the days of spring pass, continue your conversations about spring with the children. Ask them what they like and what they do not like about spring. During the conversation, help the children understand how they can help God's creation by taking care of it and by caring for the creatures in God's world. *Ecology* is a big word with little meaning to a young child, but children can understand picking up litter or planting flowers for others to enjoy or otherwise caring for the beauty of the earth.

THIRD SUNDAY IN LENT

Preparation

God so loved the world that he gave his only Son, that whoever believes in him should not perish but have eternal life.

—John 3:16

Lent is the religious season observed by Christians as a time of preparation for Easter. It is the forty days before Easter, excluding Sundays. The name comes from *lenten,* an Old English word for spring. The pattern of Lent as we know it today emerged from an earlier custom: a final preparation period for Christian converts before their baptism on the eve of Easter.

As the season developed, the emphasis of Lent shifted from the preparation of the candidates for baptism to the preparation of *all* the faithful for a fruitful participation in the sacred joys of Easter. Stress was laid on inner renewal, resisting temptation, penance, breaking with evil habits, and exercising Christian charity.

Worship

Adoration: Praising God

Parent: Give thanks to God, for God is good.
All: God gave us everything; his love is forever.
Parent: God does great wonders.
All: God gave us everything; his love is forever.
Parent: God gave us the earth and the heavens.
All: God gave us everything; his love is forever.

Parent: God made the sun, the moon, and the stars.
All: God gave us everything; his love is forever.
Parent: Give thanks to God.
(Adapted from Psalm 136.)

Confession: Understanding Us

Ask a member of the family to read aloud Matthew 4:1-11. This is the story of the temptation of Jesus. After you have read the story, talk about the temptations of Jesus and how we are tempted today. Try to identify with the three temptations of Jesus: for food, for power, and for status and personal glory. Think about how we experience these same temptations. Encourage even the youngest child to talk about what it means to have power and to be able to control someone else. Try not to point any fingers of blame or to judge any of the suggested temptations. The purpose of this experience is to understand how we are tempted in life and how we can avoid temptations, not to discover unknown sins and punish them. At the conclusion of the sharing, ask everyone to respond in unison, "God gave us everything; his love is forever."

Affirmation: Growing in Faith

Can you guess the answers to these questions: How many days did Noah spend in the ark? How many years did King David reign? How many years did the Jews travel in the desert? How many days are there from Easter to Ascension? How many hours is it believed that Jesus was in the tomb?

The answer is forty. It means "a long time," a long time to get ready for a very important event. This is the third Sunday in Lent; we are about halfway through the Lenten season. Talk about how your own Lenten season is going.

Lent is a long time for young children, and they need to see it as an opportunity to take a look at where we have been and where we are going. Talk about all the good events and those not so good in Lent thus far. Talk about how your plans to change some of your habits and your plans to do something special for other persons are going.

Dedication: Living New Life

As a family, sing or say the ancient hymn, "All Glory, Laud, and Honor," translated by John M. Neale.

All glory, laud, and honor
To thee, Redeemer, King,
To whom the lips of children
Made sweet hosannas ring.
Thou art the King of Israel,
Thou David's royal Son,
Who in the Lord's name comest,
The King and blessed One.

The company of angels,
Are praising thee on high,
And mortal men and all things
Created make reply.
The people of the Hebrews
With palms before thee went;
Our praise and prayer and anthems
Before thee we present.

To thee, before thy passion
They sang their hymns of praise;
To thee, now high exalted,
Our melody we raise.
Thou didst accept their praises;
Accept the prayers we bring,
Who in all good delightest,
Thou good and gracious King.

Living Our Worship

Choose one or more of the following:

As a family, make a large "map" of Lent. On one end write the date of Ash Wednesday, and on the other end, Easter Sunday. In between these dates, put your family's planned events to celebrate the season—worship services you plan to attend, special acts you plan to do for other persons. Talk about this map being your family's way to celebrate Lent and determine what you want to add to the map. You may want to display it.

Make an Easter lamb as a family symbol for Lent. The lamb is a symbol of Jesus, and the lamb could be placed on the refrigerator or in the center of the kitchen table. For a special Lenten meal, you might want to make a lamb cake (molds are available in most stores) for your dessert.

Make a symbol tree for Easter. The tree might be a bare branch with several twigs. Use the branch as a symbol of the cross. On the branch, hang symbols of Jesus and Easter. Consider including a cross, a lily, a palm branch, the fish, the egg, the lamb, and others. Use the tree as a table decoration during your family's Lenten meals.

Look up the customs of Lent and Easter in an encyclopedia. Pick out your favorite custom or symbol and share it with the family.

Remembrances

Go out into the yard or the woods and find a bare branch of a flowering, spring tree. The tree might be an apple, cherry, or any branch of a flowering bush, such as forsythia. Place the branch in water in a clear container so that it will bloom for Easter. Another idea is to force spring bulbs indoors for blooms for Easter Sunday.

GOOD FRIDAY

Preparation

The army officer who was standing there in front of the cross saw how Jesus had died. "This man was really the Son of God!" he said.

—Mark 15:39 (TEV)

Good Friday is the day we remember as the day Jesus died on the cross just outside the city walls of Jerusalem on a hill called Golgotha (the place of the skull). Sometimes Good Friday is referred to as Black Friday. We refer to it normally as Good Friday because we believe that through his death upon the cross of Calvary, Jesus died for our sins. This love was given by Christ so that we might have eternal life through faith.

All of us struggle with some crisis, some loss, some hurt that is our Good Friday. It is not *what* we suffer, but *how* we suffer that determines whether we will find something more that will benefit us and others.

We need to invite Christ into our lives in the knowledge that he suffers with us because he loves us and does not want us to hurt. Therefore, we need to allow him into our lives in such a way that our faith in him will lighten the sufferings of our lives through his constant and abiding love for us. After all, there can be no joy (Easter) in our lives, without our knowing hurt and suffering (Good Friday).

Worship

Adoration: Praising God

Ask one member to read Mark 8:31-38. After the reading invite the family to discuss what the message means in terms of following Jesus of Nazareth. What does it mean to lose one's life for Christ and the gospel, and at the same time to save it?

Confession: Understanding Us

Father: God, we thank you for Jesus of Nazareth who asks us to carry his cross and follow him.

Mother: Help us to remember that if we truly want to save our lives, we must lose them.

Children: Help us to show love for one another. We know this is the best way to show Jesus that we love him and are serious about carrying his cross and following him.

All: Thanks be to God for Jesus who taught us that love is the greatest gift we can give to one another, as well as to him.

Affirmation: Growing in Faith

As a family, discuss how you might help one another to lighten the burdens facing each family member. Talk about how you can help one another on a daily basis around the home.

Dedication: Living New Life

Ask each family member to decide on one task that can be done by that person for each of the other members. Make a covenant (agreement) to perform the task identified for a week, a month, or a period of time that is agreeable to the family as a whole.

Living Our Worship

Choose one or more of the following:

Using a purple piece of yarn approximately twenty-four inches long, make a necklace for each family member. Attach to the purple yarn a horseshoe nail by bending the pointed tip back to the face of the shaft (so as to make a ring through which you can string the yarn). This necklace can be worn by each member of the family from Good Friday through the next week as a reminder of Easter. The purple yarn represents the passion and compassion of Christ's love for us, and the bent nail is another reminder that each time we do something nice for one another we are showing Christ's love.

Make a cross out of nails for each family member and ask him or her to put the cross someplace where he or she will see it each day. The crosses might be hung above dressers or over mirrors.

Attend a Good Friday service in your church or community. Notice that everything on the communion table is covered in black and that no liturgical colors are present. Usually the pastor wears only his black robe as a symbol of humility and gratitude for the suffering and death of Christ. Each of us can have a good life with hope and peace because of his all-embracing love for us.

Remembrances

Gather the thoughts of each individual family member about his or her learnings and feelings about Good Friday. Use this prayer as a moment of devotions at the end of the day.

EASTER

Preparation

He is not here—he has been raised!

—*Mark 16:6* (*TEV*)

Easter is the celebration of the resurrection of the Christ, the Messiah. His resurrection proclaims the mighty *yes* in life that enables us to believe in the promise of our own resurrection. Easter does not pretend that the Crucifixion never happened. The good news is better by far. Easter builds on the crime of Good Friday and transforms it into something sacred that allows us to be cleansed of guilt and hate, both within ourselves and in our relationships with others. Therefore, no matter how you have tasted death in your experiences this past year, open yourself to a personal Easter. Christ is risen! You can rise, too. Have a wonderful Easter!

Worship

Adoration: Praising God

Father: The Lord is risen!

Children: He is risen indeed!

Mother: We give you thanks, O Lord, for giving us life and a future full of love. Let us always remember your assuring words to us: "Let not your hearts be troubled, neither let them be afraid" (John 14:27). "Because I live, you will live also" (John 14:19).

All: Thanks be to God who gives us the victory of life over death. Amen.

Confession: Understanding Us

Pray in unison the following prayer: "O Lord, help us to learn from Christ's rising from the dead on that first Easter. Help us to trust you with our lives in such a way that we are not anxious and fearful about today or any of our tomorrows. Help us, Lord, to love one another as Christ did, even risking suffering and death. Help us to show one another that we understand the message of Easter by allowing Christ's way of life to become our own. Amen."

Affirmation: Growing in Faith

As a family, discuss what you have learned during this Lenten period of self-reflection, growth, and change. Discuss how each of you can show one another and others that you love Jesus and want to follow him in a more visible way in the coming year.

Dedication: Living New Life

Ask one member to read Mark 16:1-7. Discuss as a family what the message means in terms of *Jesus going before us.* Think carefully together about the entire life of Jesus, not just his last week on earth.

Remember that Jesus said, "I came that they may have life, and have it abundantly" (John 10:10).

Living Our Worship

Choose one or more of the following:

As a family, consider the importance of the time between Easter and Pentecost, one of the most important periods in the entire Christian year. Jesus said, "As the Father has sent me, even so I send you" (John 20:21). How does Jesus intend to lead us? How do we intend to follow him?

Remember Pentecost is the birthday of the Christian church. The church stands for service for all who are in need of the love of God through Jesus of Nazareth. Therefore, the question for your family really is, What does it mean to be a part of the family (church) of God?

Create an Easter egg arrangement for the family table. Fill one dish with twelve Easter eggs representing the twelve disciples. Fill another dish with one egg for each family member.

During one of your Easter weekend meals, pass the dish containing the eggs for family members, asking each to take an egg and eat it as it comes around. During another Easter meal, pass the dish with the twelve eggs representing the twelve disciples, asking family members to take an egg and eat it as they remember the special persons in their lives who have shared the good news with them. Talk about the persons who have helped you to know and understand Jesus and his love for you. After your discussion, invite each member to communicate with these special persons about how much they are appreciated.

Give each member a bag with twelve jelly beans in it. Ask that, during the coming week, the members seek out persons who have shown them love. Ask them to give each person a jelly bean, saying: "You have loved me as a disciple of Jesus of Nazareth. Thanks be to God!" You may want to substitute something else instead of a jelly bean to indicate that Jesus loves us and that his love has touched you through another person. But please do not pass up this opportunity of telling special friends that you are thankful for their love.

Remembrances

Help your family compose a prayer for Easter Sunday that will guide you toward Pentecost, the birth of the church in your home and in the world.

FIRST DAY OF SUMMER

Preparation

From the fig tree learn its lesson: as soon as its branch becomes tender and puts forth its leaves, you know that summer is near.
—Mark 13:28

Summer means sunshine and loads of fun for everyone. It is a time when we are away from the tight and rigorous schedules of the fall and winter seasons. We are free from the responsibilities of schoolwork and all the extracurricular activities that go along with school. We are free from the hard grind in most of our working situations. We have the opportunity in summer to play and have fun with our families and to experience renewal physically, mentally, and spiritually.

Worship

Adoration: Praising God

Parent: Thank you, Lord, for summer.
Child: Thank you, Lord, for time to play together with our family.
Parent: Thank you, Lord, for children and their gift of enthusiasm.
Child: Thank you, Lord, for parents who make the time to show us love by doing fun things together with us.
All: Thank you, Lord, for summers with our family.

Confession: Understanding Us

Ask a member to read Luke 12:22-31. As a family, discuss what the passage says in terms of God's love for you and your faith in him.

Affirmation: Growing in Faith

Discuss how each of you can share more of yourself with your family. You may want to talk about ways to learn more about one another and ways to help each member accept the others. Try to find ways to practice affirming one another, accepting one another just as you are, right here and now. God affirms each of us.

Dedication: Living New Life

As a family, write a prayer that will guide you through the summer months. Use the familiar words of "They'll Know We Are Christians by Our Love" by Peter Scholtes, as your guideline.

Living Our Worship

Choose one or more of the following:

Plan a family picnic. Let every member of the family help in the preparation of the event. You may need to get out the old picnic table and clean it up a bit. Perhaps you would like to invite your pastor and family to help celebrate the season.

Go to your favorite park for the day. Take along a picnic lunch. Be prepared to take a walk together as a family and notice all the beautiful trees, plants, and flowers before you play your favorite games together.

Determine one activity your family can do at home during the week that will take a short amount of time and would be something everyone can enjoy. How about riding bikes for fifteen or twenty minutes before supper or playing frisbee?

Enjoy a great summer together with your family.

Remembrances

Make a bulletin board on your refrigerator or in some spot where the family is sure to see it. Divide the board into two categories: "Fun Things We're Going to Do" and "Fun Things We've Done Together."

Cut out magazine pictures of things you want to do. Then, when you are having fun, take pictures of your family in action and place them on your bulletin board in the category of fun things you have already done.

Once summer is over, you can use the bulletin board as a worship center for celebrating together.

Often we do much and forget so quickly. This record is one way to remember when friends ask you what you've been up to this summer.